A butterfly landing on your shoulder

by Paul Gilbert

For the wonderful people in the LBC Wise Counsel Faculty –
without their support, encouragement and love,
there would be no words for me to write:

Carolyn Kirby, Charles Grimes, Chris Parker, Ciarán Fenton,
Claire Lomas, Dana Grey, Fiona Laird, Geoff Williams, Hilary Gallo,
Ian White, John Sutherland, Jon Honeyford, Jonathan Smith,
Jonny Searle, Justin Featherstone, Katherine Bellau, Kay Scorah,
Lawrence Smith, Martha Leyton, Martin Shovel, Nicola Raj, Ray Berg,
Richard Martin, Richard Moorhead, Steve Chapman and Tina Harris.

Published by:
LBC Wise Counsel

ISBN 978-1-8383589-2-1

British Library Cataloguing in
Publication Data available.

I am very grateful for the care, design and
thoughtfulness of Jon Honeyford and Oomph Design for
their work on this and my previous books.

Introduction

As we moved from 2020 into 2021, I set out to write a weekly blog of reflections about the world and our roles in it. This book is the complete collection of my 2021 blogs from January to December. A tumultuous year of existential concerns for the world, but where the best of people shone through. I always try to write in the moment, so the blogs reflect how I feel as each week passes, but I also write hoping to keep things small enough for me to hold and not feel overwhelmed. Whatever is happening in the world that we cannot control, I know there is much that we can all influence through our own small acts of kindness, care and courage.

This isn't a collection of blogs just about lawyers or leadership, although both words appear a lot, it is mostly about how I feel we can make our difference for everyone we care about, whether they are colleagues, communities or those we love. In the end leadership is a simple idea of "can I help you?" We are therefore all leaders and all followers when we show, or are shown, kindness, care and courage.

Thank you for holding these words in your hands.

Take care. Paul xx

Contents

January 2021:

Sunday evening spin	12
...because hope alone is not the answer	14
Thinking of you	16
Call yourself a lawyer?	18
When words catch the winds of change	21
The first rule of leadership...	23

February 2021:

What counts?	28
Small thoughts in search of a big idea	30
A workshop without content	32
All that glisters is not sold	34

March 2021

It's about time	38
A time to reflect, but also to play my part	40
I sometimes wear a mask	43
"Why are you striving?"	45

April 2021

Build it well   48

Going quietly   49

A small moment carried on a kind thought   51

A space to place the times we shared   53

We can decide not to be innovative   55

The Post Office scandal – a note to your Board   57

May 2021

A further reflection on the Post Office scandal
and the three ages of an in-house lawyer   60

Earlier, Now, Tomorrow, Later.   65

Make the case and do it your way   67

The small boy in the queue...   69

May I think about it?   72

June 2021

You are amazing   76

Resigning is not enough   79

If resigning is not enough...   82

Forgotten but not gone   85

The need for speed   88

July 2021

Counting is not what counts   92
Thank you for being with me and my words   94

September 2021

Going away, to come back 98

October 2021

A guided tour of our potential   102
Muffling the sound of hate and self-regard   105
The baleful ballad of John Cocksure   107
A butterfly landing on your shoulder   110
This one is for Jane   113

November 2021

"Let those who feel the breath of sadness, sit down next to me"   118
Let your talent and potential wrap their arms around you   121
Time to be the bold architects of our future,
not the tenants of our past   123
Twelve gifts of leadership   127

December 2021

The last note   132

January 2021:

Sunday evening spin

I have treated the Christmas holiday break as would an aging bear preparing for winter.

I have laid down a sustaining layer of subcutaneous fat and would like to offer my thanks for the part played by the fridge that was once full of Stilton and cold Turkey, and also to a mountain of mashed potato, enough to sculpt Snowdonia for a winning Turner Prize entry. I have also practiced falling asleep whenever and wherever my increasingly ample exterior has encountered soft furnishings. I can honestly say that I have never been better prepared for a period of hibernation. However, as Monday 4 January 2021 looms literally just over the horizon, I suspect that the chances of falling asleep for three months and waking up in the blinking warmth of Spring sunshine, are disappointingly remote.

And so, it will come to pass that instead of escaping into unconsciousness, I will deploy my normal terrified Sunday evening routine, but with added New Year terror.

In doing so I will feign a sort of studied calm as I thoughtfully consider whether I should add to my one-hundred-and-seventy-eight item to-do list. To the casual observer there will be no clue as to my inner turmoil as I wonder if I should colour code the relative priorities described by the list. I will be like the condemned man quietly digesting his last meal, dabbing the corners of his drying mouth with a perfectly starched napkin.

Obviously the most important thing to do at such an existential crossroads is to check the cricket fixtures in seven months' time, and to ponder whether it would be better to apply for the second or the third day of the Test match. An equally pressing concern will be whether my sock drawer might need tidying. At a later point in the evening, when cricket date decisions having been made and socks have been rolled perfectly into serried ranks, I will hear the Mission Impossible theme tune play in my head, and I will resolve that not even I can prevaricate anymore, although a cup of tea would be perfect at this point.

Inexorably therefore the working New Year will begin. A time to look forward and a time to hope; however I am afraid I do not have an inside track on how to fill our boots with optimism, nor can I share with you how I intend to smash 2021 with the "New Me". To be honest I have always felt that January was a fucking dreadful month. It really does not deserve to be seen as a new start for anything. It is like the least likeable guest lingering in the corner of a party that finished hours ago.

There is for me however one sustaining thought that even a Sunday evening tango with my imposter self cannot completely shake off. While I am of course full of flaws, insecurities and doubts, I have come to realise that I do not need to be at my very best every second of every day. Life is not a competitive race where I must win at everything or otherwise lose it all.

I know I must let the world spin fast around me because it will do so anyway with or without me. My purpose therefore is not to spin with it, but to put down the best possible roots I can with family, friends and colleagues, to anchor activity with kindness and care, and to learn to bend and sway with the winds that a spinning world creates.

...because hope alone is not the answer

Is it possible for things to get any worse? Asking for a friend...

I recently stubbed a toe on the corner of my bed. Not the big toe, but the one next to it (is that one called an "index toe" I wonder?).

As soon as I did it, there was a moment before I felt anything. I surmised in this moment that it was going to hurt quite a bit; and I was not wrong. For a few seconds I chose not to look for fear of seeing my toes scattered across the floor like miniature pub skittles.

Sudden and overwhelming pain is quite a thing. There is a noticeable correlation between the intensity of the pain and the immediate need to let go of all polite behavioural norms. I soon realised, of course, that an obituary would be premature and I resolved to make a cup of tea and have a quiet five minutes.

As I hobbled into a comfy chair I started to think about the difference between sudden and overwhelming pain, and the sort of background anxiety and discomfort that comes from the times we are in today. It is the pain we feel when we cannot protect people we love, or work with people we care about, or live in the lives we hoped to build.

This quiet pain is not as sudden or as intense, but it comes with a silent and oppressive weight that pushes down on our very being. It is a tightening ligature and there is no place to scream and little comfort in a cup of tea.

These next weeks are not going to be easy, and it is not the time to paint a smile on sadness, or to rely on hope alone to see us through. Hope is indeed a fascinating, but possibly misunderstood sidekick to pain. We need it, and rely on it, and we give it lots of status; but hope by itself does not mend feelings or change anything.

The challenge for me at this time is to stay hopeful, but also to better understand why hope is not an answer on its own and yet is still profoundly important.

I am not, therefore, writing this as someone who wants to "Joe Wicks" you (or myself) out of melancholy and I do not have a swaggering metaphor to change your day. I am writing as someone coming to terms with what hope means for me in the context of my own discomfort and fears.

Being hopeful does not require me to paint a smile on my sadness or pretend that all is well; but I believe hope is real. Hope can help me find a way to live with my uncertainty and vulnerability, and to be open to the wisdom and insight these uncomfortable visitors may bring. For example, I am learning to accept that I will not get through this on my own. I know I need the care, affection and guidance of others. I know I must learn to ask for help and not feel unworthy of help. I need to accept kindness because that is how kindness thrives. And I need to be kind, because one kind act, by one kind act, is how we create a world that cares.

Above all I need to accept my responsibility to tread softly in a world of fragile but essential and wonderful interdependence.

Anxiety, pain and uncertainty do not attend alone. Hope will always be there too. The hope we can find in these days is not the antidote to our discomfort, but it is the key to unlocking kindness and courage in ourselves and in others. It means we are worthy of support and is permission for us to ask for help, as well as offering our help to others.

Thinking of you

Four years ago this month my father died. It was not sudden; he had been very poorly for some time. Thankfully, the end for him was peaceful and at home. He left us in the embrace of his three children and holding my mother's hand. I think of him every day.

As the anniversary came, and I raised a glass to a gentle and humble man, I put outside my conscious mind all the pressing moments of my world and spent a few quiet minutes just thinking about him. These moments of peacefulness that I spend with my dad, away from the noise, are as precious as ever; a shared gift from him to me and from me to him.

This year I was struck by another thought; one that is cast by the shadow of these Covid times. It is an overwhelming sense of just how precious and powerful the act of pausing becomes when we use it to think about those who we care about, but from whom we are temporarily disconnected. It becomes something precious and powerful for ourselves, but also for those who are in our thoughts..

In these distanced and interrupted times where we are denied even a simple hug to replenish our dehydrated souls, perhaps more than ever we need to make time to think about others. Such thoughts, however, should not be a glancing brush with something rushing past, or a fleeting nod to polite etiquette. It should be a contemplative and deliberate reflection that we undertake without the accompaniment of life's rude and noisy running commentaries.

If we could do this, would it not be one of the kindest and most generous acts of friendship that we could offer? Goodness me, what a gift for the people for whom we paused our world to stillness, so that they might enter a space we have made for them.

The time will come again, of course, when we can hug again, but while we wait to be back in a world where all our senses reconnect, my encouragement is to make time to honour the people we care about with the gift of making a space in our minds for them to be with us.

"Thinking of you" should never again be a half-empty throwaway line in a friendly email, typed by muscle memory. When we next write these words to a friend or colleague, it should be reporting a purposeful act, like that of an artistic curator who has been hanging thoughts and memories in a gallery of calm inside our heads.

It is an act to tell someone that they have been seen.

It says we cared enough to make time for their presence in our minds, and it offers a bridge for their vulnerabilities to cross.

It is a connection as a hug would be; because it is not the words that matter, but the kindness of the act itself, a loving and human thing that we can all practice and all receive.

As we emerge from our isolation, much will be written about what we have learned and perhaps what leadership might mean in a post Covid world. In the rush to replace, rebuild and renew our economic vigour, my hope is that leadership may also include such acts of contemplation as I have described. In the end isn't that fundamental to what leadership means? Pausing to care enough for others that they have a space in our thoughts, and where those people know we cared enough to make that space for them.

Call yourself a lawyer?

I do not often write about lawyers being lawyers. I write about them mostly as leaders, managers, colleagues and humans. However, occasionally I like to write about what it means to be a lawyer and what my hopes are for a profession that I respect very much, and indeed, a profession that I love.

It is of course a profession that includes lawyers who work in a huge diversity of roles and with all manner of responsibilities. Lawyers who work in and for Governments; who work in and for charities and who work in and for the biggest companies in the world; and there are lawyers who work for rural communities tucked away down faraway country roads. It includes lawyers who campaign fearlessly in the media, and lawyers who just want a quiet life relying on their carefully crafted precedents. It also includes those who defend and those who prosecute.

Is it possible therefore, for there to be a thread that pulls such disparate roles and people together?

I think so.

The reason we are called lawyers is because in addition to the paper qualifications and the tasks we perform, we have signed up to a set of behavioural requirements that codify (partially) what it means to be a lawyer on an ongoing and everyday basis.

For many of the roles and tasks that we perform (perhaps even the majority) we do not have to call ourselves lawyer. We could call ourselves contract managers, or conveyancers, or advisors, or nothing at all. It would not stop us doing our job or being well paid for the results we achieve. There is no need, for the most part, to add the word "lawyer" to what we do.

If we choose to call ourselves lawyers, therefore, it cannot be just for the kudos of a professional title. It is because we have given our informed and solemn consent to uphold standards that should never be compromised or diminished by a contract of employment or a client's ignorant or malign behest.

We have chosen to adhere to these standards knowing it will occasionally mean we must act against the wishes of those who employ us, and that it will always mean we hold a line above expediency, and way above illegality. It places us at some risk that in doing the right thing we might even lose work or our jobs. It is an honourable and noble tradition. Neither is it fanciful to note that in some parts of the world lawyers acting in accordance with such standards might risk losing their liberty or even their lives.

If a fellow lawyer in another land might die for their adherence to these standards, surely we do not wear the title in our more benign surroundings as a decorative medal of convenience? It means something, right?

I think it is probably the case that for many stretched and overly busy lawyers such thoughts are so hypothetical and so remote as to barely flicker in the darkest recess of their planetary sized brains. However, in my humble view, that is a moment when we are at risk of crossing a line.

I think we should routinely drill conduct dilemmas. Like fire drills or dawn raid rehearsals, we should role play in the danger zones and we should do so celebrating how it may one day save our reputations, our businesses, and the needs of the communities in which we live and serve.

2021 does not have more, or greater, existential threats than any previous year; it is just that in 2021 we cannot easily deny their existence. We know, better than ever, that Governments can lie, that Boards can cheat, and that Regulators can miss non-compliance. We know pressure can be brought upon us that bends a counsel-to-perfection into an uncomfortable ethical shape. We know we can all rush to the scene of a priority and trample over good governance in the stampede to arrive there first.

Lawyers, of course, are not the sole defenders of right against wrong; anyone can stand up and speak truth to power, and everyone can make moral and ethical choices. However, lawyers have accepted that this is part of their very identity and that it is part of their purpose to do so. We have promised.

If we do not like the gig, fine, but then ditch the title. If we accept the title, however, then we must learn to love what it means. Above all we should be proud of the fact that everyday lawyers here and around the world are doing unheralded, selfless and heroic things believing in the promises they have made; we honour their work and ours, by knowing that these are the same promises we have all made.

When words catch the winds of change

When words catch the winds of change, we do not just hear them, but we feel them too.

It has been a more comfortable week for rhetoric. Bombast, aggression, unkindness and self-immolating ignominy have flown the scene (for a while at least). In their place has come something dignified and more recognisably human. At President Biden's inauguration the words he used were very different from his predecessor, but the tone was so very different too.

Almost as soon as they were uttered the new President's words were being analysed around the world as if layers of meaning would be revealed as soon as the surface could be scratched away. I will leave others to search for meaning because I would like to search for feeling; and in doing so I will rest my thoughts on the tone of voice I heard.

For the most part I think it is rare for any listener to recall the actual words a speaker uses, the odd phrase perhaps, but what we mostly remember is how those words made us feel. That feeling can live with us forever.

For such a small word "tone" feels a little lightweight for all the work it carries on its one-syllable, four-letter shoulders, but the new President's tone was perhaps the most important part of his speech. It was measured, thoughtful, unassuming, determined, sensible and encouraging. It was not flourishing or theatrical, but on the gentler side of rather grave and with a restrained steeliness that suggested the long haul more than the short-term. It made me feel a little more secure and a little less exposed.

We also heard the soaring poetry of Amanda Gorman which she gave to us with kindness and with an amazing grace. Again, I reflect that while her words were mesmerising and haunting, it was how she made me feel that will stay with me for so much longer. For here was the embodiment of hope; a hope that was calm and youthful, but challenging, ambitious and inspiring.

It felt safe to let her words into my heart. It felt like she was giving us permission to put our trust in her generation to take care of the world.

It is obvious in a way, but the tone we set every day should be the tone that we choose to use. It should not be by accident and it should not be by chance. It is yet another way we can influence others to feel that they can relish their opportunity to shine.

The words we use matter, but perhaps they matter just a little less than how we make people feel. Of course we all want to find the right words, whether it is for a thoughtful note, or a carefully crafted report, or the opening sentences of a meeting, but from here on I will reflect so much more on how I want my words to make people feel.

The first rule of leadership...

I have had a few calls this week, and three comments stand out.

The first was a lawyer describing the time she was "let go" by her law firm at the end of her training contract. We all know that this can happen and while it is hugely disappointing it is not the end of the world. It should only signal the closing of a chapter, and in no way is it the end of the story. However, in this case, the partner who gave her the news added this:

"We just don't think you are cut out to be a solicitor".

After a rigorous selection process, and two years of service without a hint of performance management or any suggestion something was awry, one might think that the decision to "let go" would be devastating enough. Shame on this firm and this partner, therefore, who felt it was necessary to give this young lawyer a career long narrative for her internal critic to recite whenever she felt a little vulnerable.

The more I have thought about this the more cruel it becomes. Frankly, I do not care if there were technical or performance concerns (although I am sure there were none). The comment was not meant kindly and was not given as considered advice; it was self-regarding, self-protecting and a selfish act of corporate indifference.

The second comment was shared by someone who a while ago had been attending a firm's strategic retreat in some chic European city hotel. She was there as an important member of the management team, but she was not a lawyer. In a crowded room where the sound of self-congratulation hung in the air, she noticed two partners looking in her direction and then one say to the other "what the hell is she doing here".

Nice work chaps. No hint of misogyny there obviously, just bantz I expect. Perhaps they think you break glass ceilings by hurling people at them until either the glass or the people shatter.

The third comment was from a lawyer who had been interviewed on a video call as part of an investigation into the conduct of a colleague. She had no idea at the start of the call what it was all about.

She told me that she was made to feel that her failure to whistle-blow on her colleague's apparent wrongs (of which she had no knowledge) was the greater crime. At the end of the call, she was told to say nothing to anyone. As the call ended in that brutal silence only video calls deliver, she was alone, exhausted and totally devastated. There was no follow up call from anyone to see how she was, she was just left feeling very alone.

Ok everyone, buckle up.

I do not care how many industry awards your minimum-wage contract cleaners must polish in your airport lounge receptions. I do not care if you had it tougher than the kids today on your way to the top and I do not care if it is a competitive world out there and not every face fits. Please, for goodness sake, just treat people with a little respect.

I know I bang on about kindness, and I am about to do it again, but this shit has got to stop. It is no good having an award-winning inclusion initiative if you also employ gold plated knobheads who can shelter their inadequacies behind it.

Kindness is not about tolerating slack standards or accepting substandard work or indulging weakness. Kindness is your superpower. Your chance to heal confidence, to encourage excellence and to shine your light on a better path for others to follow.

Yes, we can still hire and fire. Yes, we can still criticise and yes, we do not have to like everyone, but there is never EVER a need to detonate someone else's confidence. The words we use can stay with people forever. Careless words are bad enough, but the intended cruelty of some who seem to deploy unkindness tactically or casually is unacceptable in any situation.

The partner handling the exit conversation had a chance to offer words of warmth and encouragement. He could have noted how most lawyers make their name in firms they did not train in, and he could have said he would do all he could to make her feel proud of her time as a trainee.

The partners who wondered loudly why a trusted colleague had been invited to the meeting, probably chunter over terms such as "non-lawyer" and "non fee-earner" too. They might reflect however that leadership is not about status, but about how you make those around you feel.

Investigations will sometimes be necessary, and they are never comfortable for anyone involved. However, now more than ever, without the personal networks that office life used to provide, we must be more caring, more kind and more thoughtful about the words we use. For everyone's sake we must be mindful of what happens when the video link ends and screens go blank.

The people I spoke to this week are brave and wonderful and they are all doing extraordinary things. Others may not have coped so well.

The world is tough enough, please let's make the first rule of leadership not to fuck it up anymore.

February 2021:

What counts?

What value do you bring to your role? What is the value of your contribution? Is the value you bring the value that is being measured?

The things we tend to measure, like sales, hours, fees billed and costs saved, are all important, but they are not the whole picture, they are not the whole of us.

We measure things that are easy to count. We measure economic efficiency and economic effectiveness. We appoint Finance teams to be the guardians of the data that is captured so that data can be detained in rows of cells in spreadsheet prisons. Data marshalled, projected and presented back to us as strategy; but the question in my mind is whether we are in control of the data, or whether the data is controlling us?

It all feels a little soulless and devoid of our humanity.

What if we could also measure gentleness and authenticity and wisdom? What if the numbers only counted if they came with feelings that counted too? Would we then have new role models in our businesses? People we felt inspired to emulate who were not just the rainmakers, but who made the sun shine too.

Businesses are people. If the people leave or if they cannot thrive, businesses fail. Isn't it a little odd therefore that the things we value about people (and should therefore value about business) are things we fail to count?

It will be easy to read this and say "yes, but", after all surely someone has to make the cold hard cash? A loss made pleasantly is still a loss (although I will happily argue that a loss made harshly is worse). My challenge however is not that we have got it all wrong, just that we might not have got it all right.

I wonder if have we fallen into the trap of choosing the easy things to count and then created a narrative to support counting those things? Isn't that the very embodiment of unconscious bias? What if we were to pause and count what truly matters to us?

What if we counted the integrity of our boards?
What if we valued humility, creativity and diversity in our leaders?
What if kindness and sales became a combined metric?
What if expediency cost people their bonuses?

If we were to measure the impact of our decisions on the families of our employees, would there be a greater incentive to look after our people, and for our people to stay with us?

If contracts with suppliers were more balanced, fair and shared the burden of risk, would we have better outcomes than contracts which highlight the punishments for what has not happened and may never happen?

A bullying ego is a hungry mouth to feed. Perhaps the bullies will leave if they are paid less because of how they behave and not more for the business they bring in?

I wonder as well if our colleagues would be an even more effective team if they absolutely knew in their hearts that the profits we make are the result of caring deeply about the concerns of our customers and less about random targets that a few executives created to suit their competitive impulses?

It may be harder to count joy and the difference we make through thoughtfulness, but counting another soulless binary metric seems a very poor excuse not to try.

We are all so much more than EBITDA. The humanity of our work, and the way we work, is a story that should also be collated, reported and celebrated.

Small thoughts in search of a big idea

In the UK we are coming up to a year. Hope is tiptoeing around our anxiety trying not to wake our tired fears. Thoughts dart between future plans and painful memories and we are unsure of the emotion to choose to accessorise our stoic acceptance of today.

I am carrying an awkward shaped feeling at the moment. I am wondering how we are supposed to be when we get to the other side. Should we have energetic new answers to our old problems? Or will we feel washed up on the shores of a new beginning, too exhausted to be enthused and unable to either dance or cry?

I think we are going to need a big idea. Something to help us feel that some good may come from all the mess and sadness. I think it will be important because I cannot see that it will be enough to respray our old ways with fake good intentions, or to pop "new normal" cliches like a toddler with a stash of Smarties.

When I say "big idea", however, I do not mean something preposterously grandiose. We do not need more billionaires with egos barely tethered by gravity trying, literally, to escape earth's atmosphere. No, my sense of a big idea is more about how businesses will moderate ambition to fit our real-world hopes and fears; so that we can be real people, not just corporate avatars for the next transformation strategy.

I do not have the answer, but I have a hope for what the mindset will be.

For example, our chief executives will be people who sometimes join the contract cleaners on their 5am shift, to see their work and know their names, not just their unit cost.

I would like directors to meet new joiners, not to encourage the new joiners to behave well on behalf of the company, but for the new joiners to encourage the directors to behave well on behalf of all colleagues, their families, suppliers, customers and communities.

Marketing teams will continue to create brilliant global campaigns, but they will also make time to offer a little help to local start-ups. Procurement teams will prefer to source goods and services from local suppliers, and they will share their buying power with local charities.

I want civic pride to be so much more than a photo opportunity for executives to feel less guilty about their good fortune. Businesses should be a constant presence in the midst of our communities with a desire to put something back and pay forward. Let's work with schools and care homes to offer what help we can, because once upon a time we were the terrified youngsters and, if we are lucky, we will be the anxious elderly too. Perhaps the local homeless could use our offices at night.

I know, all of this might be impractical, and none of it might work, but can we at least ask the questions?

In the end, success cannot just be about returning value to shareholders; it should begin with valuing a shared endeavour, based on doing the right thing and where we all have an opportunity to thrive.

I wonder if one day we might even hear our chief executives say, "Do you know what, I think I am paid enough, thank you", and not because they have missed some spurious target, but because they are properly connected to the 5am cleaning shift and all the other people who contribute to their success.

The big idea, you see, will not be about vaulting ambition, but about the precious smallness of us and our need for our identity to be seen in the culture and values of our working worlds. We must value our needs and our stories a little more; we need to value the analysts' commentaries a little less.

I know it has been achingly hard for too many people for far too long, but as we come through this sadness and out the other side, we will still have choices to make. The time to be better is never past; the opportunity to use our influence is always now, and the difference we make is even more powerful when it becomes the example for others to follow.

A workshop without content

I ran a workshop last week that had no content and it went quite well.

We talked about listening, about poetry, and about places and spaces that gave us peace.

We reflected on how words made us feel and not what those words had to say. We wondered how others may feel receiving our words, because meaning is not just in the keystrokes, but in the relationships we have influenced beforehand and in the fragile webbing of interests in which our words come to rest.

We talked about pauses as the buttresses for our busy lives on which we must learn to rest our weary minds. We didn't talk about the projects, the objectives and the strategies of our work. But we noticed that without the pauses the tangle of tasks tested us more.

We noticed how helping someone else to feel heard seemed to matter more to us than having something to say ourselves. To create the time and place for the words of others to be heard was to amplify our own contribution without saying a word.

It was a workshop without content.

It was a workshop about emptying crowded spaces, and allowing feelings to be felt again rather than just remembered from the past. It was about noticing the feelings of others in the peacefulness of the pauses we made when the noise would be still.

The relentlessness of our working lives is a daily test of our endurance to be resilient to the volume, both the amount and the noise. We learn to cope, to get through, and to be there at the end; but it is hardly to thrive.

My gentle enquiry therefore is to ask whether it is the content that really matters to you?

I suspect you are already wise enough, that you know more than enough to perform your tasks, and that you will achieve enough, because you strive and you care; but it is still not the content you need.

When you already know enough, the difference you make is not to know more, but in how the words you choose make others feel about what you know.

When you can do everything that is expected of you, task after task after task, the difference you make is not the next task, but knowing how to pause between tasks so that you honour your talent and fulfil your needs too.

When you have been there before and have a wardrobe full of t-shirts, the difference you make is allowing others to be heard for their potential to have its time and place to thrive.

The workshop had no content, but it went quite well.

All that glisters is not sold

If you hang around for as long as I have, you will notice how big ideas come and go, and come again. Like us, they are all just passing through.

However, for me this provides so much of the joy in my work. I love finding the ideas that inspired others. I love relishing how those ideas came to life in the hands and hearts of those who found their needs could be met through their own creative, collaborative and kind explorations. What a privilege it is for me to see, hear and understand those moments for them.

In contrast, I have often wondered why I have such a reluctance to embrace the next new "system" or "model" or "framework" that is paraded in front of us like a small-town carnival float. Then one day the penny dropped. It was not the idea that I found clunky or objectionable, but it was the energy invested in how to make money from the idea that left me disinclined to follow all the plastic slogans, flashing light bulbs and tannoyed claims.

To make money from an idea, it seems it has to be weaponised with acronyms, plastered in "roadmaps" and dressed up as a programme or program (because the US spelling is so much more, you know, compelling). An idea set adrift in a sea full of pirate resellers, with no care for a destination, just wanting the money for nothing, only the clicks are free.

The search for so called best practices can seem like this too. An idea that was special and important, born of relevancy, context and specific application, and loved by those who knew it first, but then death marched relentlessly across an organisation by a gang of project evangelists. Of course, shared best practices can have value too, but if they promote group thinking, and result in cliché laden communications dripping with confected buzzword slurry, we rip up more than quantities of cash.

In such situations hubris can take hold and it is hard for some leaders to admit they have marched down the wrong road. At worst, sadly, there is no reflection and turning back. Instead it is more likely that they will insist on carrying on relentlessly, knowing that their only refuge is at the end when they can claim that the failure is not theirs, but of colleagues who were not committed enough or who had not cared enough. Strategy reduced to a hostage video in the hands of ambitious but clueless change-makers.

My reflection is that the lasting positive difference we make is not to force-feed change on our colleagues, especially when it is fanned by vanity or the crushing need to keep up appearances. Instead when we take time to reflect and to properly understand our own intimate relationship with our everyday realities, I know there will be extraordinary ideas to be found to support our development and growth.

Successful leadership is always a collective success, albeit one that must be facilitated and mentored; it is never imposed. In contrast failure will often lie at the door of individuals who spend more time defending preconceived thinking than listening, and who treat challenge as a personal affront rather than an opportunity to reflect, learn and grow.

The next great idea could be in the consultant's expensive playbook, but in my experience it is more likely to be found in the wisdom of your team. All that glisters is not sold.

March 2020:

It's about time

This note is on time. If it's not too late.

Time, for me, has never been an ever-expanding universe that I can fill with whatever I like. I suspect time for you may feel much the same.

Time feels like a swirling wind with me trying to chase all of my different priorities, deadlines and ambitions like fallen leaves.

Having too little time, however, is not really the problem. The problem is behaving like a gambler who thinks "one more bet and I can win back my losses". The time-poor equivalent is "one more task and I will be on top of things". It would be fine, ish, if there were peaks and troughs, but in the end there just isn't time to slow down, to think, to pause or to reflect.

On a good day we can leap from task to task like free-runners jumping from obstacle to obstacle and daring not to stop. On a bad day, our online diaries are a computer screen of coloured blocks that we have let others build around us, the meeting details like Times New Roman graffiti on a prison wall of time. Either way, it isn't sustainable and we need to care to change things for ourselves.

We should not propagate apocryphal stories of people with seemingly mystical powers who can do it all and have it all. The stories that tell of some who walk among us who have mastery of their brief, who know the secrets of high-performance leadership programmes and who live in a bubble of adrenalin where being shouted at in a Californian accent on a Peloton bike is an aspirational mark of success.

My reality is of days that resemble a chaotic slalom down my mountainous to-do list, a catalogue of near misses and the odd crashing fall.

I do not believe there is high performance culture that puts us first; in such worlds we are destined to be masters of exhaustion and black belts in setting unrealistic expectations. I say again that the difference we need is ours to make.

I believe we could do more to make time a gift for others. Most meetings are not important enough to take up so much time. We must break the cycle of spending other people's time on things we know they would not choose to spend time on. We should only invite people to meetings if we know they will be needed and can make a valuable contribution. Even then, we should only invite them for the minimum time needed. We should be explicit about what they are needed for and give them permission to leave as soon as their contribution is made.

I believe we could do more to make time a gift for our teams. Some meetings should be agenda driven of course, and about business as usual, tasks, priorities, etc. However, some meetings should just be for reflection with no agenda. These meetings are for colleagues to bring things to be discussed that are not urgent, but are important. We should not mix these different approaches as they require a very different energy and mindset. A meeting for reflection is special, and what a gift that would be for hard pressed colleagues.

And I believe we could do more to make time a gift for ourselves. Once a month to set aside a day to pause. We need time to plan and think creatively about our work and our contribution. If we can, we should go off-site, meet people who inspire us, reflect with a mentor and never feel guilty that we made time to think.

I'll stop now, I know you are busy, but thank you for your time, and for spending the last three minutes with me.

A time to reflect, but also to play my part

Last week marked International Women's Day and a few days later in London a young woman's life was taken at the hands of a violent man.

It is easy to be shocked and easy to be sad, it is also easy to virtue signal on social media and then move on. I promise this isn't a hand-wringing piece about how "not all men are monsters" nor will I say how horrified I am, before going back to my comfortable weekend. Silence however is a poor choice at a time like this, and Sarah Everard's death needs more than the silence of men who choose not to reflect on the attritional burden women carry coping with male behaviour that undermines and frightens them.

In 2020 Black Lives Matter was given a tragic focus following the senseless death of George Floyd. This feels like a similar moment to highlight and confront male violence on women and other unacceptable male behaviour towards women. However, it also goes far deeper than the behaviour of some men. Our institutions of Government, of justice, of law enforcement, of education and even of health care have evolved over centuries carrying a legacy of institutional misogyny. The echoes of this may be diluted over time as each generation tries to make things better, but past decades, past attitudes and past outcomes are an overwhelming weight of disadvantage.

Today, despite progress, this institutional misogyny means there are too few women in boardrooms, in higher judicial roles, in the Government, and in certain careers. We can also see indicators of institutional misogyny in rape convictions, in the number of women in prison for relatively minor offences, in period poverty, in revenge porn, in domestic violence, in the unfathomable gender pay gap, and also in the way social media platforms protect my right to intimate, belittle and bully women under the benign convenience of my precious freedom of speech.

All of this, and so much more, is part of a compelling correlation telling us that women's interests have always been, and still are, treated as something lesser than mine. All of this, and so much more, representing the evidential narrative of structural barriers and disadvantages, mostly constructed in the past, but still with us today. A society full of institutions that were founded and managed by men in decades past that have within their DNA the obligation to protect and defend their histories, and to preserve their power today.

Layered within this societal infrastructure, like so much silt in a slow moving river, are all the everyday experiences of women who are made to feel stressed and scared about where they walk, how they dress or how they talk.

This doesn't change just because I wish it would be different, and I do not think a march or a vigil or a social media hashtag will change anything very much either. The need for change however is palpable and will happen when I accept that I must give up my privilege of being treated better than women just because I am a man.

I need to be more curious about how women adapt to a world that was built more for me than for them. I need to reflect on whether the empathy and care that I can offer is enough support, or whether because I am otherwise silent in my quiet comfortable life, I am nevertheless collaborating in perpetuating a world I know disadvantages women. I need to listen with the intensity and openness that respects the moment and the need for change. I need to be open to the idea that there must be change.

Due to Covid we have all lived through a period of historical significance. We have changed the way we work, prioritised some vulnerable and elderly souls and thrown enormous sums of money at a problem because it was the right thing to do. The lesson of this last year is that we can make enormous changes to save lives and defeat a virus. It will be hard to justify not changing other things on grounds of practicality, tradition or budget. Today we have a different benchmark of what happens when there is a compelling case for change.

History does not change at a slow or steady pace; history is changed in jolts that propel us forward beyond the gravitational pull of the status quo.

This is such a moment. I hope I can play my part.

I sometimes wear a mask

As the sun shines and daffodils appear, with all the talk of vaccines and our current lockdown lifting, I think I am allowed to blink into the Spring light with a little more hope in my heart. I feel like (and increasingly resemble) an ungroomed, dusty old pit pony about to breathe above ground for the first time in months. However, as hopes build, I have noticed that the mask I wear when I go to the supermarket, is not the only mask I put on these days.

The expected cheeriness of Spring flowers and lighter evenings is very welcome, but this also becomes a kind of mask that I can loop around my ears to cover up the sheer exhaustion of coping day to day with the waves of anxiety that lap around my optimism and good fortune. I notice it in myself, and I see it clearly in my conversations with others.

Nearly every call starts with a checklist of blessings.

"Yes, thank you, not too bad really. The schools reopening helps. The fact I may see mum in a few weeks helps too. Work has been brilliant really. We have all had hard days. I know others have had a far worse time than me. It's not easy but..."

...And so the litany of recited blessings continues, until I ask, "That's good, but how do you feel?"

At this point there is often a pause as my caller will take a few seconds to find a misplaced and neglected vocabulary about their own true feelings. Then, when they are nearly ready to speak again, I can feel a new hesitancy as their words never quite find a way to be heard, and instead a few soft tears roll from their eyes, each one carrying a drop of sadness to speak for them.

Inevitably, we then spend a few seconds apologising to each other. It is however a moment of truth; a moment when we see how just a glimpse of hope and care will find a way to pinpoint our vulnerability far more quickly than another whole day of pain ever will. I think we have learned to cope brilliantly, but when this is over, we must relearn how to be.

I see more exhausted faces now than I have ever seen before. It is a numbing emotion, and it slows us down and takes our confidence away. Small things become big things, mundane tasks stack up and noisy thoughts swirl around so we cannot rest.

We need to notice that our survivor guilt, our hard-wired wish not to complain, and our acceptance of the need for our businesses to march back to normal, is potentially the trip that might make us fall.

When I hear a phrase like "build back better", although I know it is well intended and important too, my visceral reaction is to want to run away from it and from the people who want to embrace it. In my head I don't want to build back better, I just want a rest. I want a break from feeling helpless. I just want to be with people I love and who love me; strategy can wait.

The first lesson of this pandemic should not be sought in new operating models, or clever technology, or the aspiration of business school theory. These lessons will be real, but they can wait. The first lesson of this pandemic is that we need each other more than we ever knew.

My sincere hope is that leaders will not make their first priority to launch another game-changing idea. This is not the time, just yet, for hiring consultants, splurging strategy decks, or appointing a PR firm to announce an ambitious infrastructure investment. This is a time, right now, for leaders to sit quietly with each and every colleague, to hold their hand, to ask them how they feel and to allow them to be.

I sometimes wear a mask; and I cannot wait for a time when I do not have to wear either of them ever again.

"Why are you striving?"

Occasionally I hear myself say something in the course of a conversation, and I think "that sounds quite good, I should write it down". What usually happens then, of course, is that I am distracted by something else, and later I cannot quite remember what I said.

I imagine that somewhere deep inside my subconscious mind there is a team of mining elves hacking away at a subterranean seam of densely packed detritus. Every now and then they will find a small gem which they carefully extract and then lob into my conscious mind; whereupon out pop a few words that seem to make some sense.

This week I said something which has stayed with me. I am not going to overclaim anything for it, but I will share it. I was talking to a lawyer who is wonderfully and deservedly successful. She is kind, funny, clever, liked and rather brilliant at what she does. She has also held several significant roles and her new job is big, important and entirely right for her.

Not untypically however she shares her life with someone who at best is rather grudging of her success, and at worst is a constant nagging critic. Her imposter self was in full blather when I caught up with her and there was a long list of things her nagging critic insisted she had not done, or had not done well enough.

I listened, as I always do, because I know the nagging critic does not like to be shut down, but I also know that it will eventually run out of breath. At that point, and allowing enough space for kinder thoughts to rest, I asked her "why are you striving?"

As these four little words came out of my mouth, I felt strongly that they were important. I assume that somewhere deep inside, one of my subterranean elves was doing a little fist pump dance.

In business there is always talk of targets and development and stretch and competition. In this vocabulary there is a sense of propulsion, of energy and of continuous improvement. It is however a language that is also restless and can feel exhausting.

Where is the rhythm? Where are the changes of key? Where is the meditation? Frankly, where is the wisdom?

The thought I want to share is that to properly honour all our hard work and striving, we must also allow our minds to unfurl. Otherwise, how do we reflect on all we have learnt and all we have achieved, so that we are wiser for these experiences?

Could it be that there is a point when completing one more deal, or launching one more product, or achieving one more target, matters a little less? Could it be that our value is not in narrowly repeating what we have already done, but in using all our experiences and wisdom to help our businesses, our colleagues and ourselves fulfil our collective potential to make a difference?

Perhaps if we focussed less on compiling another toppling list of tasks for today (a list that will probably not matter tomorrow) we would be able to trust our life's work a little more. In doing so we would judge less harshly every small slip or fluffed line or missed beat, and instead love the years of our life's experience, knowing we had stored away gems for our subterranean elves to mine.

I also want us to relish the thought that wisdom is not confined to the latter stages of our lives and careers. We all have our own life song to sing and to which we add lyrics and melodies each and every day. There will be wisdom in the story of our most junior colleagues, and in the new starter we have not said "hello" to yet; as well as in the quiet guy whose name we can never remember, but who is about to retire. One of our kindest gifts to anyone is to spend enough time with them to let their nagging critic talk itself silent, and to offer a space for their story to rest and be heard. We all have wisdom and we all have a story that matters.

"Why are you striving?" is not a criticism of ambition or the desire to learn. It is simply a gentle challenge to suggest that perhaps we do not always have to strive. Sometimes it is in the pauses where wisdom will thrive.

April 2020

Build it well

Now.

A place I have built made from all my gone befores.

On a clear day, now is the place from where I see opportunity blowing on the winds of hopes and fears.

Now is the time when I may, momentarily, rest the feelings I have carried this far, mostly tightly packed and hidden away, but some worn lightly so I am not invisible if you might pause while you are passing by.

Now is where I notice that this incomplete and fragile man has travelled to a point that in all the history of this world only he can claim to be his own. If I hold this moment thoughtfully, and use it well, it will always be there to lean on when later days are not as clear.

Now is just a heartbeat in an imperfect and unfinished journey, but if my heart is lucky enough to beat in step with just a part of your journey, I should not wonder how to use the moment well.

Now is the best time to say I love you, to say sorry, to be present, to listen or just to be kind.

Now will be gone almost as soon as it arrives, but it will always be one our gone befores. Our place to lean on, to draw on, to keep us warm.

We should build this well.

Going quietly

There is a constant conundrum for introverts on social media. Some days all I see is the din of opinion, the puffery of self-promotion and a constant strident flow of effluent infused self-righteous outrage. It makes it very hard to want to stay. However, at times it is also an extraordinary place to enlighten, support and to share.

I am by nature private and shy. I feel uncomfortable being photographed, filmed or recorded, and I am always nervous, even now, before a presentation. The weight of valuing every precious second that I stand in front of an audience is sometimes overwhelming and always exhausting.

In so many ways my hope is not to be noticed and not to be remembered, but just to be able to help quietly and then move on. And yet, here I am, week after week writing down my thoughts for others to read like an old school pamphleteer in a rammed town square, ringing my bell and seeking attention. It's really not me.

In my heart I know I am driven to help people to realise their potential and I am lucky enough to say that I love my work. I want to support, encourage, challenge and to offer some cover for those I help while they recover and renew. However, my internal tug-of-war, is that I have never wanted a personal profile or to put myself on a stage.

I find the very idea of the hired "guru" to be deeply unsettling. Sadly, however, it seems to me that social media is increasingly full of people relying on their modest celebrity as permission to comment in ever more strident and certain terms. At the same time, I notice that I have never felt less strident or more uncertain. It is therefore a noisy old place for someone like me and to be honest I think it is too noisy.

I love writing, but in part this is because my words are disconnected from me. I can say things that I hope will resonate and be helpful, but I want the words to be a simple gift from me to you and not to be projecting or proclaiming anything about me. I do not want to build a profile, and I do not want to monetise the sharing of thoughts and ideas, none of which are original to me in any event.

The unexpected kindness of strangers who have shared and commented on my posts has been a towering blessing throughout the last year, but I also fear I ask a lot of people who give such generous feedback. I imagine they think "O gawd, not another bloody blog"!

For all these reasons I have therefore decided to quietly allow my Twitter and Linked-in accounts to rest. I will continue to write, and I will continue to post my blogs on this website; but I will just not push them out on social media. The blogs can be found if people would like to look, but my words will not be jumping around in your timeline, arms thrust in the air shouting "me, me, me!"

Before I sign-off I would like to mention that quite soon we are starting a new adventure and we will be working again with all the amazing people who work with us at our events. I think it is going to be an extraordinary resource and I hope an important one too. It will be filled with love, kindness and care and may just be the most important thing we have ever done. I know therefore that it may seem a little odd to deny myself a social media space to tell people about something new, however I know in my heart that we will always connect to kindness and that if we keep our promise to care about the people we help, then we will always be heard.

Please continue to visit this website to read my blogs. Please give me a call or drop me a line at any time. Please come to our events when we can hold them again and please know that we will always offer a quiet place to listen and to help if we can.

Social media has been an extraordinary gift to the world in so many ways, but it is not for everyone and I know it is not for me. I hope we will always be able to connect, but as humans and not as avatars. I will always, always love to hear from you. Please take care. Please be kind. With love.

A small moment carried on a kind thought

When I was seven and in Mrs Davies's class at St John's primary school, I wrote a story about our family caravan holiday. I mentioned the sand sculptures on Weymouth beach, and I got a really low mark. I asked Mrs Davies if she did not like the sand sculptures. Her "what-on-earth-are-you-talking-about" face suggested to me that she might not have read my story very carefully. I wonder now if this was the first time, but almost certainly not the last, when something I have written has been read by precisely no one at all.

If you are reading these words, even if you are here entirely by accident, thank you for coming. On Twitter or Linked-in a few hundred people might see this post, but here there will be just a handful of us, perhaps enough to sit around one small, imagined coffee table. My words and your hot drink of choice.

I like the thought very much that I am talking just to you and that we are in a quieter space where a gentle thought can linger.

I love how something can become less important, but at the same time become more special. The smallness of the moment, if it is carried on a kind thought, matters so much more than a grand gesture or rhetorical flourish carried on a need to be noticed.

We seem to live in a world where being seen has become more important than being together. I want to push back against that idea. I would prefer, for example, to have a mentoring conversation where we can sit close and focus on being present and listening, than to make an amplified presentation to hundreds of people in the grand ballroom of another identikit conference hotel. In a mentoring conversation I can hope to help you in a way that is personal and meaningful to you, but in the ballroom presentation I can only hope not to bore you, as I look out upon row after row of mostly anonymous faces with half an eye on their phones in any event.

I would like my writing to be more like a mentoring conversation. I want to write small, so that it is just me talking to you and no one else. Writing for an audience is not what I set out to do, because it becomes something else; it becomes about projecting onto a perceived expectation and in doing so the quiet intimacy of a fragile thought is lost.

In a mentoring conversation there is a sense of calm and of truly valuing the thoughts we might share because only we will hear them. While I cannot recreate that feeling in a blog, I hope my words this Sunday morning might encourage you to pause and to find a peaceful place to be with the sound of your own true thoughts. If we can tune into their rhythm and cadence, and allow our thoughts to rest and breathe, I am certain we will find all the wisdom that we need.

Then we must hope for the courage to listen to our wisdom.

I hope it is a courage we will love finding and will never lose. It is an empowering feeling that is far away from the din, far away from the performative and far away from the look-at-me culture that is all around us. It is in this courage, found by listening to our wisdom, that we can value the soulfulness and meaning of our needs.

We all know that we cannot succeed on our own for long, however if we are to find the people who can help us on our way, we must step away from what others expect of us and project on to us. Then, when we are truly comfortable with what matters to us most, kindness will find us and it will be easier to accept.

Take care and thank you for being here with me now.

A space to place the times we shared

A dear and precious friend of mine has lost his dad very recently.

In a year, and in a world, of so many sad things, one more sad thing might seem to have less consequence. It has however, touched me deeply. It has also made me stop and think about the feeling of loss and what replaces it.

My friend's dad was called Lew and I met him only three times. Each meeting, however, was at a cricket match and for those of you who may not understand the significance of this detail, such days are never short and can never be forgettable. A day at a cricket match will always unfold in all its simple, gentle, burbling pleasure, with smiling souls bound together in hours of friendly conversation, in wonderment at our blessings to be there and in beer, as well as occasionally reclined in slumberous repose. It is a bonding experience of the very finest kind.

Having met Lew only three times, you might think it would be a little strange for me say I loved him, but in a way I did. He represented Dadness for me in a way I have not felt since losing my own father four years ago. He was thoughtful, kind, and had a twinkle in his eye that spoke for a love of life. However, the twinkle was held in a clasp made of a working man's wisdom. He was strong and resolute, and with a moral compass that would never let him down. Perhaps above all I loved the obvious pride he had in his children and grandchildren. I felt Lew would never be the centre of attention, but somehow he would always be the centre of affection.

It is a special thing to give the world your presence in such a way that those who meet you feel safe and good about themselves. It is an even more special thing to give those people memories and feelings that will, in part at least, fill the space you leave behind.

My grief for Lew is of course a drop of rain in the storm of loss that my dear friend and others will feel about him for the rest of their lives. Even so, there is a gap that Lew has left for me too, and yet it is now a space I can fill with his memory and the memory of the times we shared. I will never again walk into Edgbaston on the morning of a Test match, and not think of him. The first beer of each day in that wonderful ground will always be "to Lew".

I hope this does not sound flippant or trite, but perhaps the loss we feel when someone precious leaves us is not a gaping hole into which we must endlessly pour regret and feelings of loss. Perhaps instead it is their final gift to us, the space in which we can lovingly place each fond memory, every small kindness and their timeless wisdom; a space to reflect on all that they gave us during the times we shared. We may be destined to miss them every day, but we are left with treasures made of love.

R.I.P Lew and thank you.

We can decide not to be innovative

Being innovative is a really bad idea in most situations. In most situations relying on tried and tested is best.

I accept entirely that if you had been on Apollo 13, running out of air, but with a cardboard tube and some chewing gum, then that would have been a very good time to be innovative. However, if you find yourself in months to come in a meeting room on floor 13, a bit bored and with only Post-it notes and a transformation consultant for company, you do not need to be innovative.

The myth of innovation is that is it always a good thing, but it isn't.

Again, I accept that if you have just invented a vaccine for Covid then this is super cool innovation because otherwise we might all die. However, if you are in a legal team spending months figuring out a way to automate a document nobody reads and carries a risk rating a notch under "that would be a bit irritating", you are not being innovative.

The often oppressive requirement in performance indicators, appraisals and in procurement processes for individuals, teams and suppliers to "be more innovative" has wasted more time and caused more anxiety than any other three-word phrase in the history of corporate bullshit bingo. It is lazy FOMO.

I am convinced that there would be much more innovation if we all told our colleagues "look, whatever you do, don't be innovative". Why? Because we like to feel confident about what we do, we like to feel motivated to do stuff, and we want to do our jobs well. Frankly, when that is how we feel, that is when innovation is more likely to happen.

I was reminded this week of some wise words my granny told me when we were on a day trip to the seaside, circa 1968. I was a painfully skinny child with pipe-cleaner legs and ill-equipped to embrace the Baltic weather that gripped the near deserted beach. I reluctantly paddled in freezing ankle-deep water in my hand-knitted swimming trunks, but Granny could see I wasn't really enjoying myself and came down to the water's edge to reassure me. She told me "if you want to get wet, jump in. If you want to tit about on the edge, carry on as you are."

It has made me wonder about the relative importance we put on innovation and decisiveness.

Management mandated innovation is characterised by its near guaranteed baked-in pointlessness. Innovation is needed when we have to make do and mend; or when we are together in unchartered territory. Innovation therefore comes from living with a compelling necessity. However, in a world where you can hire consultants for £3k a day to massage the corporate ego, and take comfort breaks to buy cappuccino, innovation becomes just another way for businesses with more money than morals to incur expenses that reduce their tax bills.

Decisiveness on the other hand is such a crucial skill to practice. It speaks of our competence, humanity and moral compass. To be decisive is to exercise judgment. If we can do this applying our years of individual and collective wisdom, by analysing the available facts, consulting with those impacted and reflecting on what is the right thing to do, then that surely is worth investing in and developing.

The next time someone's bright idea is that we all need to be more innovative, please think of my granny and the more useful need for us to be more decisive instead.

The Post Office scandal – a note to your Board

In the light of the Post Office prosecutions scandal, this is the email I hope every in-house legal team will consider sending to their Board and Executive colleagues now:

"Dear Colleagues,
The miscarriage of justice caused by the Post Office –
where were the lawyers?
This message is sent on behalf of everyone you employ in your legal team. We all approve this message and ask that it is read with the same care, respect and kindness with which we have prepared it.

Everyone in our business will have seen and read about the Post Office prosecutions scandal. No doubt there will now be repercussions for those executives and lawyers who were directly involved. We will not judge things too quickly before all the facts are known, but what is absolutely clear is that there has been a shocking miscarriage of justice. The lawyers and executives who were most closely involved have the most serious questions to answer about what they knew and how they behaved.

The role of lawyers in any business, including your lawyers in this business, is to protect your interests expertly and fearlessly. However, the role of lawyers can never be just about carrying out the wishes and directions of their employers. At the heart of what all lawyers do is to explicitly and diligently uphold the administration of justice.

No matter what the business imperatives or the pressure we all feel, we hope you know and welcome that we will not be silent if we need to raise concerns or objections to a decision, policy, behaviours or course of action that undermine our duties as lawyers.

We are proud to be employed here, and we hope you are proud to support us in fulfilling our role.

Thank you. Your legal team."

May 2021

A further reflection on the Post Office scandal and the three ages of an in-house lawyer

...A further reflection on the Post Office scandal and the three ages of an in-house lawyer

I have observed and worked with in-house lawyers ever since my very first day as an in-house lawyer on Monday 2 January 1989. Then I was a wet-behind-the-ears new recruit starting out in a now forgotten business that it was my good fortune to join.

My career as an in-house lawyer was carefully parked on the side of my expected career path in the year 2000. That was when I left my second GC role and went walkabout to find a new adventure. I have never been back, but instead for the last 21 years I have worked with in-house teams the length and breadth of the UK, across Europe and from Singapore to Cape Town to Chicago, mentoring, presenting to, and consulting with in-house lawyers from all backgrounds, of all experiences and in teams of all shapes and sizes.

That's nearly 33 years of close observation and I have decided it is high time that I write down my reflections about the profession I love. I will share more with you about my plans in the coming weeks, but I want it to be freely available and to build over the course of this year and next. I want to share all that I can to let others find the things I hope might help them in their journeys too.

That's for the future, but for now, for today, I want to reflect some more on the Post Office scandal. For some background please read Professor Richard Moorhead's quite brilliant "Lawyerwatch" blog and the extraordinary journalism of Nick Wallis set out in his book "The Great Post Office Scandal".

There are grave concerns relating to the decision-making of executives and lawyers. It is possible, of course, that the Post Office lawyers did all that they could and this should not be ruled out in the understandable rush to place blame. Lawyers can also be bullied and feel threatened, and lawyers can feel overwhelmed with pressure.

While I am not looking for people to blame, it is impossible not to see the catastrophic failure of leadership and its crippling impact on innocent families. It seems utterly bewildering that at a time the Post Office was inflicting such pain and suffering on so many people, that other Post Office employees, no doubt kind, thoughtful, competent and empathetic souls, could all be going about their own work oblivious to what was happening. This includes of course the in-house lawyers.

How can this be?

In my opinion, many in-house lawyers work in structures that are bound to fail when they are put under significant pressure. These structures are nearly all self-built by the lawyers themselves, driven by the demands of the moment rather than foresight and strategy. As a result, nearly all carry a small, but inherent and all too predictable risk of collapse.

For the remainder of this blog, I will explain how this happens. In doing so I know I am oversimplifying the analysis; I will therefore write about these things in much greater detail as part of the work I have mentioned above.

There are three ages of an in-house lawyer. It is a sort of progression, although many lawyers stay stuck in one age that either suits them temperamentally, or where the culture they work in demands they know their place. My observation is that each age has the potential to be benign and positive, or to create the circumstances for epic ethical failure. The three ages are:

1. Seeking acceptance
2. Promoting convenience, and
3. Making a difference.

Seeking acceptance.

This is the stage for newbies and idealists. We are all here at some point. This is the age where lawyers put relationship pleasing at the heart of their efforts to feed their need to be liked, to be valued, to be noticed and included.

In this age, there will be much talk of lawyers needing to be commercial, of never saying "no" and of going the extra mile. Lawyers will say that service is everything and that they must be outstanding at meeting the requests made of them, whatever the priority it truly deserves.

At one level it is harmless and cheerful, but it is also limited and risks becoming pathologically subservient. At worst it indulges, appeases, excuses and facilitates harmful outcomes. Seeking acceptance has a value, but it is too easily exploited and only really works when everyone else plays nicely. Lawyers should never be so naïve.

Promoting convenience.

Seeking acceptance creates demands that in the end cannot be met, but most in-house lawyers believe that their personal inconvenience is a sure sign that they are truly needed. It is a kind of winning.

In-house lawyers create dependency. Becoming indispensable is just a higher level of seeking acceptance. However, even the most ardent exponents of this approach will, at some point, realise that something has to change. Their winning is now placing increasingly intolerable demands on an exhausted and limited supply of lawyers.

When told they can no longer simply grow their teams by recruiting more lawyers, they will often become evangelical for the importance of technology and better process. Done well this can work incredibly smartly; a place of genuine purpose and efficiency. However, done poorly and the outcome is lawyers stuck in an unrelenting cycle of still having too much work, still having too little resource and now with the additional distraction of trying to build resilient infrastructure. Their eye, very firmly, not on the ball.

Making a difference.

For some lawyers, the need to break away from the grinding bind of too much demand and too little resource, becomes overwhelmingly seductive. They have got a little bored of trying to restructure, reprioritise, refocus and of running efficiency projects that never end. Now they just want to be more strategic.

I am not decrying the need to be strategic because all teams should be. By being strategic they can make their difference. If lawyers get this right, we see the superstars of the profession, lighting the way to guide us all and leaving the world in a better place. The problem is that too many lawyers arrive at this moment escaping from their past inadequacy and have no clue what "being strategic" really means. For them it tends to morph into a flaccid desire to just "be in the room"; and lo and behold, by wanting so much to be in the room, they are back in an instant seeking acceptance.

Each of the three ages is two-sided. Each age offers wonderful days and fulfilling careers where talent can flourish, and a lasting difference is made. It is where my love of this profession comes from. However, each age is also its own subtle and blind-siding trap. Great care is needed to be vigilant and strong. Hubris, complacency and arrogance will find you out.

I will say this until the day I die, but I do not care for your operating model, or your clever tech platform or your excellence awards, if you downplay or fudge the fact that the most important reason to be an in-house lawyer is to know when to say no when everyone else wants to hear yes.

If in-house lawyers walk by on the other side of this fundamental truth, a significant percentage will become susceptible to failure. Within this group a small number will be bound to fail. When you fail, your career, and potentially the lives and livelihoods of others will be ruined.

The blog I wrote last week, with the draft letter from the GC to the board, affirmed this essential role of the legal team.

The blog resulted in an email from someone I know to be a brilliant lawyer. She told me:

"I especially like your letter to the business from legal in light of the post office scandal. I wonder if we can summon up the courage to do it. It seems doubtful."

The GC, of course, is not bound to fail; but in my eyes he has become susceptible to failure.

I say again – the most important reason to be an in-house lawyer is to know when to say no when everyone else wants to hear yes.

Earlier, Now, Tomorrow, Later.

Earlier

We were all standing slightly apart from each other on Tuesday. A quietly shuffling group of people, and a cold wind forcing hands to be pushed deep into coat pockets. There was obvious and understandable melancholy in the chilled air. I looked for little moments of recognition between the people arriving and those who had arrived already. Funerals are not a place for conversations, just for weak smiles, an exchange of knowing looks and for eyes filled with the realisation of loss.

This close to the end, there is no comfort in grief, it is raw and unyielding. Nor will grief let you feel another's pain, it only reminds you of your own. However, listening to the tributes for a dearly loved man, the room began to fill with memories that are already a gift of comfort and gratitude. When a family photograph caused an audible chuckle, the sadness for his absence was now wrapped in the warmth of his memory. A life cannot be described in just a few minutes, but if we allow time for fond memories to be recalled a whole life is appreciated. The difference we make is not in the things we acquire and bequeath, but in the memories we share with those for whom we care.

Now

The world turns, even though we want to pause; deadlines loom and people will inevitably step into our line of sight with their issues, concerns and problems for us to solve. It will always be hard for us to make time for ourselves, but that is the purpose of memories. Memories tap us on the shoulder and catch us in the moment. Memories take us to places where we do not have to pretend and we are uniquely real, where we remember how others have made us feel. We are not made by the workaday tasks we complete, but we are shaped by the memories that we create.

In memories there is the influence of those who we have shared something precious with us. Their care and example are now in our manner, our tone and in our deeds. We should not therefore memorialise the shape of a man or count his property as telling us anything of note; but beyond their days, we are their legacy, a reflection of their love and of their ways.

Tomorrow
Typically, work is a to-do list as long as our arm, with back-to-back meetings and immovable deadlines placed to scupper our hopes for time to plan and think. For some these things are a badge of honour, but for most of us they are a straitjacket on our time to be ourselves. There is something soulless about such days, filled in this way.

Tomorrow's course is already set, and if we are not careful each following day will be just like the last. It is therefore down to us to ensure that each day includes small acts of kindness and gifts of love. The most important thing we can ever do is to make a memory with someone that they will carry long after the moment has passed.

Later
On Tuesday we left a lovely man to rest in peace. When our light dims, and it is our turn to be the reason people gather in our name, shuffling in the cold and eyes filled with sadness, I hope we will be remembered for the light we have given to others. What a wonderful thing to still be part of their journey with the memories that we made together, and which will now accompany them forever.

Make the case and do it your way

It was probably about four years ago deep into a parched rainless summer. After a stiflingly hot, slow Tube ride and then a longer walk than was ideal in a city where the sun's heat bounces off glass and is stored in pavements to burn your feet, I arrived at the door for an event hoping more than anything for super efficient air-con and a chance to lean against a marble pillar.

He, on the other hand, arrived in a chauffeur driven Mercedes S Class with tinted windows and the whiff of maturing LTIPs. I heard him tell his uniformed driver to be back in sixty minutes, he would not stay for any networking. With that he walked briskly and purposefully into the building. I watched this little story unfold with a bystanding couple who had paused and wondered out loud who the important person might be. As I pushed on a door that should have been pulled, I wondered briefly about my life choices. I used to be a GC once you know; had I stayed in my role would I now be driving around in a big black "fuck-off" limousine?

I was there as part of a panel that had been assembled to discuss a hot topic with hot takes. The panel discussion was memorable only for one remark made by the S Class GC. The moderator's question was something like "should GCs be on the board?"

It is an old chestnut and there are good points for and against, but my answer has always been frankly, no. The S Class GC however spoke at length, sharing all different styles of importance, ending with "Who would want to be a GC who was not on the board?"

I am always a little lost in these moments. Partly I marvel at the ease with which some people can run off a cliff of self-awareness fully expecting that their granite-like confidence will overcome a mere immutable law of nature like gravity. And partly I am caught wondering if my almost imperceptibly raised eyebrow and studied pause conveys quite enough "FFS. What. An. Absolute. Arse."

The future of in-house lawyers is full of possibilities, but I would like to suggest that the S Class GC might not be the apogee of our evolution, more a variant of the species – Homo Erectus Knobus.

My observation, however, is that for every S Class GC there are a thousand others who every day have too much to do, too little time to plan, too little resource to be fair to their teams and, unsurprisingly, too little energy to fulfil the potential for their role. These people might aspire to be on the board one day, and that should be their call in their context, but what they need most is space to think, plan and to lead.

In my view, Homo Erectus Knobus is an ethical risk. Their independence is swamped in gold cards and platinum access. For the rest of us, who arrive hot, sweaty, irritated and tired, hoping for the air con, the difficult question is whether we might be an ethical risk too. We are not blind, or wilful or wear tailored suits woven from freshly mown hubris. We know our role and we know we must be courageous too, not least because every day we fight our small battles for our business and our teams; but we are also weakened by the environments in which we work. We make do, we accept more for less, and we always hope that next year will be easier than the last, but it never is.

A metric of our success is not whether we saved up our minor illnesses to coincide with our annual leave. Avoiding burnout is not a mark of how strong we are. I also fear, more than ever, that hindsight will not be our friend if one day we discover that the air con was not super efficient, but was just a fan awaiting the arrival of a crock of flying shit.

Our role is not to play the heroic underdog, nor obviously the prized tit, but the space between is our compelling reason to be; a place to make our case of which we are certain. To have no regrets.

The small boy in the queue...

On Tuesday 18 May 1993 I left home in the chilled darkness that hangs in the air before the dawn chorus. When I arrived in North London, at the home of Arsenal FC, it was just after 7am.

There was a bleary-eyed throng of people outside Arsenal tube station. The low sun was not yet warm, but it was cheerfully picking out the vivid red and white in old faithful scarves. As I looked up Highbury Hill past the cherry blossom trees, I could see that a queue of people had already formed in front of the ticket office. They were standing three deep across the pavement, perhaps around five hundred people in total. Their purpose, and mine, was to secure a ticket for the FA Cup Final replay on Thursday night at Wembley Stadium.

The ticket office would open at 10am, but thankfully it was a dry, bright morning and while the queue was mostly silent there was a sense of achievement and of common purpose. In our heads we had counted how many people were in front of us, and we all knew we would get a ticket.

As I stood in the queue, alone with my thoughts, I was proud of making the effort. This is what proper fans do, and I felt like a proper fan. I was literally with my tribe, outside the stadium I adored, knowing that all I had to do was wait. In a few short hours I would hold an FA Cup Final ticket in my hand and I would be part of something important forever.

In 1993 I was not a kid; I had been a qualified lawyer for six years and an in-house lawyer for four years. I was married, mortgaged and a new dad. I was a grown-up. Kind of.

There are fixed points in one's life that mark the passing of time – going to college, getting a proper job, getting married, buying a house, perhaps having children – each step denotes a maturing of the child into the young adult and on into something properly grown-up, stable and responsible. As I stood in the queue however I was a little boy again. Hope filled my heart. The feeling of belonging to something far more important than me was almost overwhelming, but so was the sense that I had the right to belong. This pavement, at this time, in front of this beautiful old stadium was where I was meant to be.

Now it is May 2021 and as I sit at my desk writing these words, two things feel very powerful to me. The first is how comforting it is to have a true, deep and shared sense of belonging. The second is how we all have a child inside us that we need to love and honour, so that this child may guide us throughout our adult life.

We all need to belong – to our church, our family, our work, our profession, hobby groups, our sports teams or the communities where we live. It is about having shared memories, and being part of something bigger than us, but still being needed all the same. It is also about our place, our contribution, our values and our roots. It is the thread to a past that we can hold in our present and it is the same thread we know others will hold in the future as well.

If a small patch of pavement in North London, where I once stood with strangers, can evoke all of this, can you imagine what an extraordinary gift it would be to help others have a sense of their belonging too?

When we belong, we are not alone.
When we belong, we matter.
When we belong, others care that we are there too.
When we belong, our potential is given a reason to thrive.
When we belong, the child inside us is safe.

This is so important, because the child inside us is the hope we need for our future. If we can love the child within us, this love becomes the opportunity to wonder again, to be inspired, to feel the enormous possibility of life and of our lives. This love means we can suspend logic and disbelief and let hope be our guide. It allows our feelings to come to the surface to breathe rather than forcing them to be cloaked in common-sense and pragmatism. It is to dream.

Standing in a queue on a pavement, the small boy inside me was holding a dream I had held my whole life. Arsenal won the FA Cup two days later, but it isn't the result that matters, it is the fact that I was there, and I will always be there. I belonged in that moment and that moment will be with me forever.

In our world of work, we have all manner of policies for diversity and inclusion, but a policy for inclusion is never enough on its own. It is why we must be continuously vigilant to help everyone feel more than just included. It is our responsibility to help people feel that they belong.

A policy for "diversity and belonging" would have so much more power and love than a policy simply to include.

The lad who wanted to be a lawyer who came from a humble home life, who only went to a Polytechnic and who somehow found a training contract in a country town general practice, always had a hill to climb if he was going to feel he belonged. A little while later that lad was mixing with chief executives and general counsel, and he was even more uncertain if he belonged.

I do not think I have ever said this before, but understanding these thoughts has helped me come to terms with my role as a mentor and guide. I suspect I have always carried a feeling that I did not truly belong in our wonderful and extraordinary legal profession or in the higher echelons of corporate life. I never really felt worthy enough, and as a result I suppressed my child within.

When I am working as a mentor, or if you come to our events, I sometimes sense this feeling in others too. In a way it has become my life's work to help people feel that they can truly belong, and to allow their child within to be their guide and inspiration for their potential, forever.

May I think about it?

It was just another ordinary day. I was probably three weeks into my first General Counsel role. The calls and messages of support and congratulations had passed. This call was from a director looking to create some fancy new entity to buy another company.

Me: "Can I come back to you; I need a little more time to think about it?"

Director: "No, we don't have time; I need your answer now."

Me: "I don't have all the information I need, and I would prefer to think it through. I won't sit on it, I promise, I just think we might find a better way."

Director: "Of course, there may be a better way Paul, but you're sounding like a lawyer again. There are only two ways. Do we go ahead now, Yes or No?"

(BTW, the word "again" in that last comment still runkles my equilibrium).

This conversation, and versions of it, happened most weeks. As a newly promoted General Counsel I was suddenly in the middle of established, but unfamiliar ways and my daily terror was not having time to think.

The combination of hard-wired executive behaviours and myriad unseen informal networks where information flowed all around me, but was largely unseen by me, made giving an opinion feel more like playing hopscotch in a minefield. The corporate mindset was strong, but hid in plain sight. My struggle was how to take a grip of my role and not feel that I was either whitewashing half-built walls or delaying the best idea ever while I pondered the shade of grey opinion that suited the moment best.

I still worry about some of the things I did decades ago. None of it off-the-scale TV-worthy drama, just the everyday tug-of-war between my conscience and pragmatism. For example, was I strong enough with an over-zealous policy on debt collection? Or did I do enough to call out one executive's bullying mindset? With hindsight, I should and could have done more. It still niggles way.

The privilege of middle-age hand-wringing however is deeply unattractive, so let me get to the point.

Every day, in every company someone, somewhere does something dumb, inappropriate or troubling. Sometimes lawyers will have a chance to influence these things and, if we can, we should try to pause and hopefully stop any nonsense. Sometimes however we will turn a blind eye, we may even acquiesce. In the gathering rush, in the relentless noise, and in the narrow windows that we look through, we cannot be everywhere, see everything or have the energy to intervene each and every time. It isn't ideal and we know hindsight will not be our friend, but very (very) rarely does it have anything to do with lacking moral courage or failed values.

Stuff happens EVERY day. We all know it happens EVERY day. I used to find myself standing in places that made me feel intensely vulnerable or irritated; or which seemed totally chaotic, or where it was too late to change course. That however was the gig. I now have twenty years of mentoring experience and I know it is still the gig for huge numbers of lawyers, all over the world.

So what is to be done about it?
In a way nothing is to be done about it. The power-plays, the nudging boundaries and the flatulent ideas that are given their wind because others are cheer-leading the next big thing, are the realities of corporate life and they are as certain as the chief executive's bonus. However, because we know these things are certain, we should not let anyone go into a General Counsel role who will be surprised or unprepared. We need to normalise the fact that there will be ethical pressure. This does not mean we need to treat in-house legal departments like a crime scene, but nor does it mean we should shrug our shoulders, look the other way, and busy ourselves with marking up another routine contract.

I have three suggestions:

First, we should put the role of the General Counsel on the risk register. This is not because the General Counsel is a risk, but because if the business puts her under the drip, drip, drip of ethical pressure, then at some point the business is at risk. I know she can resign if it all gets too much, or if she is professionally compromised, but surely we have the imagination to de-escalate concerns well ahead of such a moment?

Second, as a matter of course, any General Counsel leaving any company, in any circumstances, should be interviewed in private by the Chair and the Non-Executive Directors. Her views on risk, resources, ethical pressure, relationships and on the challenges facing her successor should be transparent and clear to all in the boardroom.

Third, the General Counsel should prepare an annual report for the Audit Committee on how she and the Legal Team are resourced to meet the needs of the organisation they serve, and how their structures and priorities are aligned to the needs of the business.

If I were a GC today, I would welcome these suggestions. They would make me feel less exposed and better supported. If you have read this however, and think it is unnecessary because you are strong, experienced and your company behaves well; may I please ask you to pause and to consider if your talent and your good fortune are things that we can all rely upon.

June 2021

You are amazing

You do know you are amazing?

A story in the making, full of joy, sadness, hope and vulnerability. An inspiration, even if you feel small and incomplete.

How do I know? Because it is the story of all of us. We all have our amazing life story. Of course, it is easy to hide behind "no one will care" or "but, I have done nothing really" or "not compared to what she has done", but that is true of all us too.

I love your story. I know this even without knowing you, because I know it will hold truths and ideas and adventures and missed moments and lost loves. Whatever feels ordinary for you, your story will always have the capacity to inspire others. More importantly, when you need it, your story is the soft blanket of reassurance you can wrap around your shoulders when days are less comfortable to bear.

If I am helping people to reflect on change, or to cope with moments of stress and discomfort, I often start by asking them to write the self-reflective story of their career thus far. The highs, and lows, the feelings and the moments that shifted gear and changed their worlds. The stories then told, I promise you, would inspire anyone. The stories also seem to give purpose and momentum and reassurance for what is happening now, and for the adventures to come.

Every week I sit with my laptop to write my blog and I look at the blank page. I want to write because it is a sort of therapy for a swirling mind. Inside my head I can feel the discordant sounds building in volume. It feels like the noise an orchestra makes warming up before a performance. I know that each sound is hopefully useful and lovely in its way, but when they are played over each other, they become a tumbling din. Writing for me calms the din; it separates the strands of noise and allows me to see the colour of a sound and hear the harmony in a thought.

The blank page therefore has become one of my favourite things. My safe place to calm the noise.

I also see the blank page as a metaphor for my work. Each new page, like each new day, is a place of hope and opportunity. A place where there are no mistakes, no clunky lines, no misunderstood messages – just boundless possibilities for words to nestle together in colours of meaning. A chance to start again, and an opportunity to notice the new stories of love, loss and endeavour that I recognise in the amazing people I meet every day.

The blank page is also a chance to literally pause. We are all rushing by in a world that is rushing by. A trillion data points every second. It can overwhelm us and wash us away. Learning to tell our story is an act of kindness to ourselves, a way to slow down, hold on and to feel we belong. A blank page will willingly accept all our words. Each word with its own reason to be, placed by our hands, to honour and reflect the meaning of our thoughts.

I love the thought that everything ever written, every story ever told, every lyric, every play – literally everything – started with a blank page. Every writer who has made a mark on our conscious minds, or shaped our world, started that process with a blank page. It is the same starting place for us all, without hierarchy or preference or privilege. It is our opportunity for our story to be given form and substance and a direction for ourselves and others to see.

Whatever has been written before, by you or me or anyone else, there is always a new page that can be started. We are not constrained to only follow; we can create and shape new ideas or we can bring new light to established thinking.

As soon as we make the first keystroke the blank page will always be our most forgiving friend; we can start, delete, edit, start again – we are never judged and we will always be offered another pristine page to gently lay out our hopes, fears, ideas and challenges.

You do know you are amazing?

The joy of knowing you, is the joy to also reflect you in my words. The small things we walk by and forget before we have even noticed, might be the moments that hold back the tears for others, or which shine a light when darkness descends. The path you have trodden is also a direction for others to follow.

What would it be like if we treated each day as a blank page? What if we noticed meetings and events and relationships as part of our narrative and allowed them to tell our story? What if we told the story of how we felt so that others could hear our needs and not have to guess them or care less? What if hearing our needs was permission for others to speak up too?

What if leadership was not always strategic and far off, but small and in the moment? What if you then used the moment to tell your amazing story?

Resigning is not enough

...The Captain then made her usual pre-flight announcement. As she handed over to the cabin-crew she reminded us that her colleagues "are here for your comfort, but mostly for your safety, please give your full attention to the safety demonstration, even if you are an experienced passenger".

It is, in its way, the perfect purpose statement. The same message is given to each passenger at the same time and given by the person who we all recognise to be in overall charge. The statement also makes explicit that however much she expects the cabin-crew to make us feel comfortable, there is in fact only one true purpose – to manage our safety, especially in a crisis.

Over many years now I have contributed to the conversation about the role and purpose of in-house lawyers, but in the last few weeks the Post Office scandal has rocked me to my core and forced me to look again at what I have said. I have not done enough.

I have always been concerned that professional ethics is downplayed and placed somewhat ambiguously in a lawyer's hierarchy of needs. Being a good person who works hard and who tries their best is not the same as purposefully advocating for the resources, access and influence to ensure there is an effective ethical and governance infrastructure. Being part of the inner circle and regarded more as a business partner than as a lawyer, for me is not a mark of success, but a sure sign that ethical pressure will be harder to notice.

The safety valve in the debate, on both sides, has been that if anything really untoward happens, the lawyer can always resign. We all agree on this point, so the debate gets lively but is then allowed to cool in a cul-de-sac where nothing changes.

I do not believe we can let this continue. Now something must change because I do not believe resigning is enough.

In the Post Office scandal we know the following things:

- There was an aggressive contracting regime that placed the Post Office in an overbearingly powerful position to declare shortfalls as debts owed by colleagues.
- There was an aggressive prosecution strategy that created an environment of fear and isolation.
- There was a deliberate strategy to thwart independent investigation and to hide (and destroy) disclosable materials.

We know therefore that the governance systems, policies and processes, and the people who managed governance oversight, were weak, incompetent and/or colluding in activity that resulted in the biggest miscarriage of justice in the UK, ever.

This happened over many years. It was not a one-off event or a series of sad/bad coincidences. This was ethical failure on an epic scale.

This was an abuse of power with the purpose of preserving a corporate reputation and the corporation's value, even when lives were needlessly destroyed.

The chief executive, chairman and directors are responsible, but so are all who supported and encouraged their decisions, or who looked the other way.

Resigning is not enough.

People have died, families have been ripped apart, people have been made bankrupt and gone to prison for years, having done nothing wrong.

Resigning is not enough.

The duty of the General Counsel is to act at all times in the best interests of their client, subject to the rule of law and the proper administration of justice. At its core, this is the equivalent of the Captain's pre-flight announcement. If it were to be given by the chief executive it would be in these terms:

"The General Counsel and her team are here to ensure your deals are done, your contracts are fair and to help make your business decisions as seamless as possible; however, above all, the legal team are employed to be part of our governance framework and their first duty is the efficacy, legality and moral legitimacy of all that we do. Listen to everything they say and follow their guidance please".

I also note that the Captain's announcement is made on EVERY flight without fail. It isn't said once at the beginning of her career and after that we all hope for the best.

I do not see any urgency in the legal profession for General Counsel to assert their primary purpose. Instead, we have legitimised an institutional complacency that seems to put commercial expediency first. We have created environments where we have to be liked in order to thrive. We value relationships over making a difference, and all too often mental fatigue and burnout are an occupational hazard where the quality of decision-making may have been compromised.

My concern in not to punish, but that we learn. We operate unsafe systems and resigning is not enough. We all have to step up. This includes law firms, in-house teams, executive directors and non-executive directors.

We know that an emergency landing for any aircraft is thankfully rare. We know that the safety announcement is a little tired and many of us can tune out when we hear it; but deep inside we know that every flight is an endeavour that carries the risk of death and, for the airline industry the risk of catastrophic reputational harm. The Post Office scandal is rare and awful, but lesser versions of it have happened before. "There but for the grace of god" is not a strategy that is in any way good enough.

If we have any influence at all, and if we care about our colleagues and our profession, we need to reflect and learn. I also believe we have a duty to every poor soul impacted by the Post Office scandal to be certain of our most important purpose, and that we have the Captain's unequivocal message of support announced routinely for all to hear.

Resigning is not enough.

If resigning is not enough...

"Do you expect me to talk?"

"No, Mr Bond, I expect you to die."

A few days ago, I wrote about the Post Office scandal.

I made clear my view that resigning is not enough, but some people have rightly challenged me to say what I feel would be enough.

I have been asked, for example, if lawyers should become whistle-blowers. I think this is problematic for the vast majority of situations, but I do not rule it out entirely.

Some people have asked if I think there should be more regulation. Even if that might help, it is clearly contentious and would be a divisive debate. To be honest, if our current professional conduct frame was respected more (frankly even, known about more) there is enough guidance to help us. I also believe there is enough goodwill and wisdom in the profession to sort this out now without more regulation.

In this blog I set out some modest steps for every in-house lawyer to consider. My points are suggested for debate. I am not saying I am right, I am just asking that we engage with the issues and address them. We must come at our responsibilities not as if we are the indignant accused, but as custodians of a great profession that society needs to be an exemplar of leadership.

My hope is that we can look at proportionate and pragmatic ideas that will help save us from falling into difficult places, rather than how we punish or write despairing blogs when some inevitably will fall.

Contract of Employment

The contract of employment for every employed lawyer should explicitly reference their professional rules of conduct and state that the employer will honour, respect and facilitate the lawyer's obligation to comply with their rules of conduct.

Incentives

No lawyer should be remunerated in such a way that it will likely cause any reasonable person to question their independence or the motives for their advice. Where there is a Remuneration Committee I think it would be prudent for this body to set the General Counsel's salary and incentives.

Scope and Resource Reporting

The General Counsel should report to the Audit Committee annually on the scope of their role and especially if there are things which are not in scope for the resources at their disposal. The General Counsel's report should explicitly confirm that they do have the resources necessary to discharge the work that is within the scope of their role.

Access to the Non-Executive Directors

The General Counsel should meet routinely in private with all non-executive directors to discuss her work priorities, risk and reputation, including any instances where she believes there is inappropriate ethical pressure.

Conduct risk

The combination of too few resources, overbearing management pressure and inexperience is a theoretical but significant conduct risk. We should calibrate it, monitor it and report on it. We may not like doing so, or consider that it is incredibly remote, but we do not like floods, fire, terrorism and cyber attacks either, and they might also be incredibly remote. I am only asking that it is considered a risk, not that the General Counsel is a risk. When an organisation today considers its risk of cyber attack, it does not turn a blind eye because it might upset the IT Director.

Exit interview

An outgoing General Counsel, no matter the circumstances of their departure, should meet with the Chair and other Non-Executive Directors when leaving the organisation. I would also welcome the newly appointed General Counsel meeting the Chair and Non-Executive Directors shortly after their appointment for an initial and in-depth briefing on the Board's and the General Counsel's expectations.

Seeking allies not isolation.
In many companies and institutions there are multiple governance roles – The General Counsel, Compliance, Co-Sec, Risk, Audit (etc). This should be a group that can consider, reflect and challenge. We should encourage these people to do so, a collective and coordinated endeavour, not silos of good intentions.

My closing thought for this blog is that ethical pressure is often only obvious in hindsight. However, this must not be our excuse to do nothing now. Instead we must make it our incentive to be thoughtful and creative and to use our brilliant brains to ensure we do not have to look back in despair, but that we look forward with pride in what we stand for and how we do it. We are not James Bond, and we do not have to be, if we work on this together.

Forgotten but not gone

Social media is an odd place. It has been, and often still is, a cheerful distraction, full of insight and generosity; and it can be an extraordinary force for good. However, it is also a place for confected rage, pointless stridency and shallow promotion.

My Twitter profile says I joined in May 2009, and that I have 3318 followers. The language is seductively clever, isn't it? The word "joined" offers that sense of club and community and a place to belong. While having "followers" permits a mostly harmless self-regard for our own opinions on everything from croissants to climate change. I am absolutely certain however, that in any other part of my life, if I spoke of "my followers" the response would be a deserved awkward silence, at best.

I may have joined Twitter in 2009, but I joined the real world in 1962. Sometimes I feel I belong there and sometimes not. As for followers, on most days I am confident of only one and she is a cockerpoo called Crumble. My real world does not indulge me like my virtual world, but I know my place in it and I know I am blessed.

Earlier this year I decided to come away from social media for a while. I did not find the decision very easy, and I often think about what might be happening there without me. Not so much a "Fear of Missing Out", more a "Fear of no one noticing I've gone".

(I guess FONONIG doesn't quite trip off the tongue like FOMO).

I was however undoubtedly overinvested in a facsimile community, in the certainty of opinions and in the weird currency of followership. These are all good reasons to take a break. A chance to reset and reflect. A chance to be forgotten, but not gone.

I have an increasingly clear view of my purpose (which at my age is about time!). My purpose is not to build a vantage point from where others can see me, but for me to use the experiences and insights of decades of observation to help others see themselves more clearly.

A perfect day for me is one where no one knows or cares what I do, but where I know that a quiet thought, shared with love, has helped someone take a single step towards owning their full and amazing potential.

A little earlier I mentioned the opportunity I am taking to reset and reflect. A chance to be forgotten, but not gone. I would like to develop this thought a little more with you if I may. I think there is something here for all of us.

I think it might be especially important if you have ever found yourself between roles or if you have been on an extended break through illness or perhaps a maternity leave. These periods can make us feel a little lost. We are separated from teams, colleagues, buildings and the rhythms of our working lives. We also learn how everyone can cope very comfortably (a little too comfortably) without us. We know we are missing out on the in-jokes, the small talk, the gossip, the usual irritants that bond and the shared highs and lows of success and failure. Absence is a chilly and muffled separateness than can sap confidence and leave us feeling outsiders in a world that used to be so familiar.

I know this is how it can feel, but I also believe that being forgotten but not gone can be a powerful and rejuvenating place for us to be. You are not validated by your job, if anything your job is validated by you.

If we believe in our gifts and if we accept that we are always only lending our talent to our employers, then in the inevitable periods when there is a break, there is precious time to replenish our depleted energies. We can smooth off all the barnacles of office life and reconnect with our values and dreams. We can find again the nervous anticipation of new adventures and learn to love the opportunity for renewal. To be forgotten but not gone is not something to dread, but perhaps a blessing in an otherwise relentless world of work. My encouragement is to embrace its offer and love the journey that will then unfurl.

In a small way, my time away from social media is a time for me to be forgotten again. I can still write, still have calls, still meet people, but without looking over my shoulder at 3318 avatars and doom scrolling a timeline that tells me everything is rubbish, wrong or a puppy.

If you are between jobs, or if you are on maternity leave at the moment, and if you are feeling separated and a little lost, please try to relish these days. It will not be long before you are once again loaning your wonderful gifts to somewhere new (or back where you were before). This time, however, with fresh thinking and all the new colours of experiences and insights that you bring from the perspective of a space and time which allowed you to step away and be yourself.

There is anxiety when we are separated from our familiar world of work, but often the anxiety we feel is from other people around us. Well-meaning family and friends only wanting the best for us, but often they are projecting their insecurity rather than reflecting ours. I am not suggesting we can be selfish or cavalier with the needs of others who rely on us; but a break from the habitual and the constant pressure of the moment means we can step aside for some much needed renewal.

To retreat, to be forgotten but not gone, to reconnect with all that we are and all that we offer the world, might be our temporary and essential place for perspective, self-love and growth.

The need for speed

The need for speed pervades all we do.

We are bombarded with advertising and influencers wanting us to lose weight fast and be beach ready in 14 days. Or the new FFSx that will do 0-60 in the blink of an eye, ensuring envious looks from those with beach ready bodies. Or mega-fast broadband, that allows multiple devices to be open at the same time.

The breathlessness of it all is sold as exciting and better, but I find it all rather daunting. Actually, it mostly sounds like hell on earth.

Some of my anxiety is, I know, overdeveloped and reveals certain insecurities that I should not masquerade as truth. I know that in my whole life I have never had a beach-ready body, it is now best described as a beached body. If seen from a cliff top vantage point, most people would call the local sea-life sanctuary in the hope I might be refloated on an incoming tide. My antipathy to people who want to drive fast also spills over into my aversion to running. I am convinced there is no such thing as a fun run. My longstanding advice to all runners is to please leave earlier and enjoy the stroll, and in doing so avoid frizzy hair, sore nipples and pants that runkle. As for digital stimulation, are we not already living in a sort of digital Bedlam, where cacophony is described as information?

Why is doing something more quickly synonymous with doing things efficiently?

I spoke to someone this week who calmly and rationally told me that they simply did not have time to reflect and plan. All he could do was to hope to get through the day navigating the slew of emails and meeting requests that had broken away from their tethering and were hurtling towards him like recently cut timber tumbling downstream through boiling rapids.

I asked him how I could help, and I heard the usual conference agenda bingo – we need to be more strategic, we need to make better use of tech, we need to be better business partners, we need to...

I told him that I didn't think I could help. The concerns he had for his work were not the concerns I had for him and his team. He was spinning in his wheel, and the faster he ran, the more he just stayed still, but with added exhaustion.

I told him he needed to do three things, just three things, but each would be difficult and each would need him to ask for some help.

Action #1: He had no boundaries. No red lines. Anyone could call him, email him, disturb him at any time. He considered it part of the job to always be on call and available and ready to help. He thought this was what good service looked like. Ironically, he didn't expect this from his team and wanted them to have balance and boundaries; but what he did not notice was that his team felt less able to have boundaries, because of the way he behaved. They followed what he did.

I told him to sit down with his team and agree team boundaries which he would adhere to as well.

Action #2: He had too much on. He had allowed (even encouraged) demand for his time to outstrip the practicalities of the resources available. He was constantly asking for more people and more tech, but never showing how the business would benefit, and always being given less than he needed. It was an unbreakable cycle in his mind and his only solution was to continue to work ridiculous hours at the cost to his mental health, his family, friends and to his career.

I told him to sit down with his Chief Executive and Finance Director, but this time not to ask for more people or greater investment. This would be a meeting where he would tell them what he was going to deliver and what he was not going to deliver with the resources he had. This is not admitting failure, it is being a good colleague and leading your team.

Action #3: He had no time to plan and even to think. Saying you want to be more strategic, but them adding this ambition to the agenda of a team meeting under AOB in the last 15 minutes of a two-hour meeting is not going to achieve it.

I told him to have one day a week (still just 20% of his time) to have no BAU related meetings and to answer only crisis emails. These days are going to be precious days. They are not for him to indulge flights of fancy, but they are an investment in the business helping to create a sustainable and important contribution. The days will include conversations with peers in other organisations, time reflecting with members of his team and time with his thoughts.

None of these things are easy because they require him to change his behaviour and that is why he needs help. I am certain however that what he doesn't need right now is more tech, more people or to go even faster to keep up. The need for speed pervades all that we do, but often we succeed best, when first we can bring the spinning wheel to rest.

July 2021

Counting is not what counts

Legal Department metrics? I am not that bothered.

Count what you like, present it how you like, extrapolate it all you like, the things we count have largely been chosen because we can at least count them. This is like measuring the dimensions of a canvass because we do not have the vocabulary to describe the picture.

The difference we make does not come with an easy to see, easy to explain, tick in the box. It is a shame, but true, so we end up counting stuff that doesn't really matter, pretending it does and making everyone around us feel just a little bit complicit in the charade of the empirical's new clothes.

I think I was eleven years old, and I had just started secondary school, when I asked my maths teacher "if zero means nothing, why is it such an important part of maths?". A wonderful conversation followed about maths and value. If something cannot be counted and yet still has value in a subject like maths, why are we so hung up on counting things when our subject is about judgement, doing the right thing and the law? Surely, ours is a story to tell, not a number to crunch.

Let's not count pointless things anymore. I really do not care if you have a dashboard of many colours. The things I care about are the things we find almost impossible to count. Do people listen to you? Are you and your colleagues kind? Do you have influence when it matters? Is it safe to speak up? Have you understood the ethicality of your purpose? Does your business care that you have the access and the resources you need to thrive?

The right answer is rarely just a number that we can count, but it is about how we make other people feel, and how they make us feel. What is better for you (a) an acceptable answer in the context of an outstanding relationship, or (b) an outstanding answer in the context of an acceptable relationship? And where would you prefer to work given that choice?

Throw away your metrics. They are an administrative distraction that you have cobbled together to make you feel more connected to the sales geeks and finance wonks who live (or die) by what they can count. My advice is that you should absolutely care about their numbers as if they were your own; relish getting to know their meaning and their effect. However, do not invent your own numbers and then pretend they matter to you just as much. If you do, you risk becoming the needy kid who wants to be loved for putting colour on your spreadsheets and imagining you now manage risk more effectively as a result.

Throw away your metrics and tell your story. You are the contribution that cannot be easily counted, but which allows everyone else to do what they must do. Some days you are the invisible "zero", but without you, the company will fail as surely as the mathematical formula will also not work.

Throw away your metrics and tell your story, because we all know that one courageous and kind intervention may transform the life of a colleague or a client. And we all know that this will count far more than all the contracts you have ever templated and that no one ever reads.

Your story is facilitate and prevent; it is to be involved and to be independent; it is to love and to criticise; it is a world of complex context, interdependent relationships, momentary influence and myriad behaviours. Your story is not a number. Your job is not to count, but to be counted.

Thank you for being with me and my words

A letter between friends is a rather old-fashioned idea, but one that still carries a sense of something a little more thoughtful, personal and caring. The act of writing a letter is imbued with warmth and the gentleness of something shared. It isn't ordinary.

I know this message isn't a letter, it is just another blog, but I would like it to be a letter. I would like to be addressing these thoughts just to you, whether we know each other well, a little, or not at all. The fact you are reading these words is a special thing for me and I thank you so much for taking a little time to sit with my sentences and to make what you can of my thoughts.

I am writing to you because I am conscious of two significant disconnects. The first is how little time we have spent in each other's company in the last 18 months. A time when it has been so hard to reflect with each other and to be at ease with a half-thought or just a silence. The second is how social media (a gift in so many ways) can drive division by the oversimplification of complexity and then insisting, in effect, that we must choose a side.

Both these disconnects can result in a simultaneously lonely and noisy background when our lives already lack too little company, too little peace and not enough reflection.

I received an email this week from someone I do not know, who took the trouble to kindly and politely take issue with some of the things I have written. I reflected that it was a privilege to receive his message, but also that I was sad to have added to the noise in his life.

It made me realise (again) that there is a responsibility we all carry in the messages we share. A responsibility not to just add to the noise. While respectful debate is an invigorating experience, and a good conversation is always wonderful, if we are projecting opinions for no gain, save for a mild sense of "hear me, hear me", we might reflect that it is not the kindest thing we can do.

It is of course important to feel heard, and I am convinced that to listen is one of the kindest things we can do. However, to throw more sound on the bonfire of cacophony should always be done with care for others. No one wants to be poked in the chest with another unwanted opinion.

So, this is my letter to say that for the next few weeks I am taking a break from writing my blog. I will be back writing again in September when with your help and care I will try to offer thoughts which I hope will resonate, but never divide us.

In the meantime, my hope is that it will not be too long before we can be together, enjoying the richness, joy and uncertainty of simple conversations that spark and wander in wonderful unplanned ways; and where personal opinions matter far less than the sense of simply being with people who care to share a space and time to listen and to encourage everyone to be heard.

I hope you have a wonderful summer and I hope we may meet soon. Thank you for being such a kind and willing companion for me and my words.

September 2021

Going away, to come back

I wonder if these keys work.

My laptop is open, and a blank page awaits, I have not written a blog for a few weeks now. I can hear the computer fan whirring away as if the engine is running, but not yet in gear.

Writing has always been my way out of darkness. Sometimes, seemingly from nowhere, an idea will swing into view, flooding the page with light and I have to quickly scramble over what it shows me in case the light dims. Sometimes there is only a flicker of something that might be a half thought somewhere in the distance, and I have to trust that if I walk towards it, the light I think I can see will become worthy of words.

For a while now, too long, I have not seen much light. I have worked normally (for the times we are in) but my world has been dark. I have wondered if it was time to stop. I have had a good run and been lucky beyond my imagining. Perhaps it is time to fade away and be content that others will now have their time, as I have had mine.

But here I am, writing some words again because last week I stood on a stage and welcomed delegates and friends to our first residential event for two years.

I began, as I did two years before, with a Terry Pratchett quote. His words invite reflection, and offer the hope of fulfilment and growth:

"Why do you go away? So that you can come back. So that you can see the place you came from with new eyes and extra colours... And the people there see you differently too. Coming back to where you started is not the same as never leaving."

In this moment, being with people who had come away, my darkness lifted a little. I knew we would see the colours of ideas and feel the rhythm of conversation. I knew we would share again, and I felt able to learn again. Most of all I felt the strength of being beside people who care. Learning doesn't happen just because we receive information; learning happens when we open our minds to the possibility of our growth and trust others to help us on our way.

Our world talks of "pivot", and "hybrid", and challenges our sense of relationship with video calls where we look at people but may not see them. Life moves fast. Innovation and change are part of our lives forever, and part of what it means to be us in our world. To learn however, is to pause and the perfect place to learn is together.

Through this time of our lives, defined by the challenges of a pandemic, we have all been away from what we knew and found familiar, as we come back I hope we will see extra colours and find opportunities in them to make our difference to the things we care about and for the people we love.

October 2021

A guided tour of our potential

"There are signs of recovery, with an accompanying sense of normality, in the conversations I am having with people going for new roles and being excited about the possibilities of their potential and for new adventures to come.

It feels like an awakening from a deep, deep hibernation. It is heartening for an old timer like me to see optimism in the eyes of good people; however, one slightly downbeat note is how dully formal, banal and unimaginative job interviews can still seem to be, often sucking the joy out of an opportunity. While it isn't worthy of a full-on rant, it still leaves me a little sad that interviews are too often such cautious and under-explored meetings.

I would love there to be much more energy, challenge and exploration in this process; and for the objective to be less about not making a bad hire, and much more about making an absolutely brilliant hire. With a degree of impertinence that only comes without responsibility, may I suggest a few questions for both interviewers and interviewees...

Questions for the employer to ask:

- What are the qualities you bring to this role that make you feel proud, and how would you like to work with us so that these qualities can be seen and felt by us?

- How would you like to be managed and what are the leadership qualities you most admire in others?

- When you find yourself a little out of your comfort zone how good are you at asking for help and what will we notice if you feel stressed?

- How do show kindness to colleagues? What will we notice that shows the importance of your kindness?

- When was the last time you achieved something that made you feel truly fulfilled? What were the different emotions and feelings you had at the time?

Questions for the candidate to ask:

- What is the best contribution I can make for you at this time, and how will you help me make the best contribution I can?

- On a bad day, what am I likely to see in those who manage me and those I work with?

- What is it about my CV and my story that makes you think I will be a good fit for your team and your plans?

- I know I won't be the only person who can do this role, and I hope you have a great list of candidates to assess, but if I was lucky enough to be offered the role, what is your best advice for me to succeed in my first few weeks?

- Nothing is forever, so there may be a future date (hopefully far, far away) when it will be the right time to move on. How can we work together so that we will know we gave our best to each other?

So, nothing outrageous or gimmicky, but things that get to the heart of our humanity and especially our need to do well for others and for ourselves.

Too often people talk about hiring as being a bit of a lottery, and perhaps my questions do not help change that possibility; but interviews should be an opportunity to make every candidate feel hopeful about their potential, energised by the ambition for the role and needed. If we held this thought at the front of our minds, I think the interview process would become instantly more engaging and valuable. A job interview is a guided tour of our potential and of the role we hope to fill; it is a moment to relish what we have achieved already and to be hopeful for what is to come.

Muffling the sound of hate and self-regard

There were a number of reasons why I came away from social media earlier this year.

In part, filling my mind with the relentless sadness and struggles of the world had started to feel overwhelming. It didn't matter if it was one person's loss or a planet in crisis, it was hard to see how I could help. However, even more than this, was being a witness to a timeline where pettiness and bullying sat ignorantly, arrogantly and all too noisily with grief and empathy.

When something savagely awful happens, like Sarah's murder, timelines mark our sadness and horror, but then respectful and reflective commentary is all too often drowned out by those who wish to shout their own agenda or spike kindness with something noxious and dark.

I resented, and still do resent, the uninvited intrusion into my mind and I ache even more for the pain it must cause those who are vulnerable and more directly involved. While it is easy to shut one's phone or computer, once seen it is so much harder to remove the bleak unkindness which corrodes goodness and blurs decency. I decided to walk away for a while, defeated and sad.

Now, however, I have tentatively stepped back, not because it is better, but because pretending it isn't there is not the answer either.

As I post again, three things are guiding my thoughts.

The first is to use my voice and not to be silenced by the noise others may make. I don't mean by this that I am some paragon of virtue or that I must be heard; I just mean that I want to support, encourage and care for the people and concerns that are important to me. My silence would not help them, which isn't fair to them or to me.

The second is a realisation that has come to me late in life, that I do not have to change the world and be disappointed when I fail.

I can however influence a few individuals to find their voice, trust their talent and to explore their potential. I no longer seek to be the voice of anything, or to have a big unifying idea, or to say anything original ever again. But I do want to reiterate that kindness, and the opportunity to be kind, are available to all of us, even in the smallest of moments. Twitter and Linked-in are not for me a platform to grandstand, but a space to support, to listen, to offer a little hope and to help where I can. If I stopped using these platforms completely, I would deny myself an outlet for kindness, thoughtfulness and to show that I care.

The third is to be a counterpoint to the hate and the poison. There is an apocryphal story you may know well of a little girl who walked along a beach with her dad after a storm. Thousands of little starfish had been washed up by the storm and were now stranded. The little girl painstakingly collected one at a time and returned them to the water's edge. After a while her father said that she could not save them all and it was time to go home; but the little girl said in reply, "we don't have to save all the starfish, but we can save one more". If there is a seemingly endless capacity for some to hate, let there also be our own limitless capacity to share, care, love and support.

I suspect we should all take a break from social media from time to time, and I know I will need another break one day. Together, however, we can make kindness a relay of caring thoughts carried with love and then passed on. Leadership, in social media terms, is not the strident view, but about letting others be heard whose voices are soft and hesitant. In these ways we can at least hope to muffle the sound of hate and self-regard.

Sarah may you rest in peace, and may your family and friends find some small solace in the kindness of strangers who do care.

The baleful ballad of John Cocksure

"I fundamentally disagree" said John Cocksure, shaking his head in the exaggerated manner of someone comfortable in the limelight of their own making.

He then lolled backwards on his chair, his legs stretched out in front of him and slowly placed his hands behind his head. The sweat patches under his arms confirmed the whiff of practised posturing that was now filling the room.

My first thought was to try and remember what on earth I had just said, because even after all these years, if challenged I am still likely to assume I must have said something stupid.

My second thought, as I looked upon his casual slump and his studied "now I have your attention" manner, was to recall past moments of similar challenge and it is rarely a moment of insight and inspiration. Only a certain type of man engages in this self-indulgent look-at-me shithousery. Indeed, I reflected afterwards, that in thirty-five years of being with lawyers, I have never ever seen a woman do this in a training session, at an event, in a client meeting or a team meeting.

I invited John Cocksure to elaborate a little, perhaps using words rather than performative body shapes.

"I just don't believe what you said is true."

I had a choice at this point; whether to accept that every opinion is valid, agree to differ and move on, or to dive headlong into the rabbit hole of possibility (despite the evidence in front of me) that John Cocksure might be in charge of a functioning brain and therefore had something interesting to say.

The point I had been making just before his head-shaking and wet armpit display, had been that at some point in our careers all lawyers will face an ethical challenge. Some will notice and react, some will notice and choose not to react, and some will not notice at all.

It turns out that John Cocksure has never had such a challenge and never will. He mostly knows this because he knows his own mind and besides, you can't make an omelette without cracking eggs, and business is business, and because "what-ifs" don't get deals done.

As the morning unfolded, you may be surprised to learn that John Cocksure found it hard to accept he might be wrong about anything. The more categorically something came out of his mouth, the more obviously right he must be because he trusted his gut.

He held forth often and each time the room fell silent. His colleagues knew better than me that life was too short to engage in a debate. Not only was he sure he was right, but because of the silence around him he was also sure no-one disagreed with him.

This is perhaps excusable in the poor souls who shout on buses, but as he was a senior lawyer in a significant company, I was pretty appalled. His General Counsel told me after the session that John Cocksure was a really good business partner and that the business loved his certainty and bravado. He described John as someone who was a better leader than manager, and someone who created energy in the room.

I described John as a "significant conduct risk" and a "bloody nightmare."

I suspect I might not be invited back, but then I have always felt that if my work had to be lashed together with expedient flattery and ego-washing, it would be a leaky old boat to set sail in.

The issues with John Cocksure are clear and obvious, but they are also clear and obvious to his boss. The General Counsel has therefore found a way to excuse the behaviour and so the behaviour has become normal.

I hope John Cocksure is everything positive his boss thinks he is, but even if the General Counsel is right, the negatives should not be ignored. His "energy" silenced the room. His opinions were ignored because he himself never listened, and he ruined the opportunity for conversation, reflection and collaboration.

It is the General Counsel, however, who is the more significant problem, because under his leadership his team are adrift in their own self-silenced indifference. The height of the team's ambition is to get through the day. No learning, no growth, no change. A slide into mediocrity with only the baleful sound of the ballad of John Cocksure for company.

One day soon John Cocksure will fancy himself as the General Counsel. I suspect he already thinks himself better than his boss. Thank goodness there will be no ethical challenges for him, as he brings his energy to the room.

A butterfly landing on your shoulder

As summer allows us to slip from her grasp, we turn up our collars and look to find our way through the cooler mists and softer lights of autumn. I know that I am also moving into the autumn of my career. A time therefore to make the most of the light in each day, to reflect, and hopefully to share well.

I have loved my work and still want to do more, but it is also a time for others to move into their rightful place, to shine their light and to shape our futures with love and care. I know, more than ever before, that the difference I will make now is not in any grand design, or polemic assertion, or even to say I know best. My difference is in the quiet space between decisions, where there is time for me to take your cares and offer them a safe place to rest.

To have arrived at this point has been over thirty years in the making. It was thirty-two years ago that I was promoted to my first leadership role, and recently I have been thinking more and more about what I know now compared with what I didn't know then. I would like to share a few brief thoughts.

I promise I do not live in a Pollyanna paradigm, but in the same frustrating, inefficient and bureaucratic world we all know too well, however it is my strongest wish that we learn to unconditionally love our teams. It is because the world is like it is, that we must give our colleagues our very best. It is a privilege to care for their needs, to honour their differences and to challenge their potential to give of their best too.

Conversely we should care a little less for the corporations that employ us; it is the people who matter – our colleagues, our customers, and our communities. The thing to care about most is doing the right thing by them. It helps therefore not to over invest in the idea that organisations care; we are units of economic utility, with a spreadsheet

value for now, that is all. Well meaning statements about vision and values can be important, but they have been designed as avatars for the good times. They are what a business hopes it is in a benign and airbrushed universe.

A great role in a great company is a butterfly landing on your shoulder. It should be cherished in the moment, but not expected to last forever. Our indelible mark therefore is not made on a CV of illustrious brands, but in the difference we make to the people we lead. This will stay a vivid memory long after a company, or deal or project is forgotten.

How should you be therefore, if all this is to be achieved?

Speak when you should, not just when you are invited. You do not have to speak often or loudly, but you must respect your own values and you must show you care to defend them and to promote them. Speaking up takes courage. It should be practiced on the small things, so that it is easier to do for the big things.

Remember that behaving to meet your needs is the start of meeting the needs of others. You must become your first and best advocate. Do not outsource hope.

Trust your judgement, but also practice using it. Saying after the event that you thought something wasn't right, just means that you were wrong too. Leadership happens when we try to influence people and events in the moment. Hindsight is a threadbare comfort blanket for those who choose which side they are on after the event.

When you are wrong, the least you can do is apologise. The best you can do is change. Your journey will be full of mistakes and moments when others feel let down. Tread gently, but know you can always grow if you recognise when there is a need for you to change.

Life comes with some pressures that we can predict and many that we cannot. You will be tested; however, you are not defined by the place you work, but by the values that guide you. Let your values show you the way and never be pulled into dark corners by events or people who have allowed themselves to be caught out by expediency.

Help others shine their brightest. We are never in the shade just because the light is not our own. Step back when your work is done, step forward when you can help others be their best.

You will never feel entirely comfortable that you deserve to be in the right place at the right time. However, be careful not to play small. Never let your gratitude for your good fortune be a brake on your development, or stop you challenging what should be challenged. You are not an imposter, or about to be found out, but you have an independent mind, open to the possibility there is more to learn and to the unexplored potential of the difference you will make.

I am certain that you know enough to succeed. Knowing more is rarely the answer. For most of us it is how we use what we know that is more important. Your gifts therefore are ready to share right now. Never tire of being kind, you cannot waste kindness, or run out of moments when it makes a difference for others.

And a final thought for those days when you cannot be your best and you may even feel overwhelmed. Take time to pause and allow yourself to be loved, and know that this is the same world you have helped to make, a world where people love you and care about you too.

This one is for Jane

What should we expect of the most senior lawyer employed in a business, or charity, or public institution in the UK?

She is called Jane and she is a thoroughly decent, hardworking lawyer. She is professional, kind and respected by her colleagues. Jane is of course her employer's lawyer, and her job is to work for her employer's best interests. However, in a very significant way Jane also works for us.

You might have views on the types of business Jane works for and you may not especially like that it could be an arms manufacturer, or a Saudi wealth fund, or a business about to open new coal mines, or one which has great relations with government officials in China. However, this makes it even more important for us that Jane can do her job well.

Jane's duty is to do her best for those who pay her wages, but she must also do so in the context of her wider professional responsibilities. These duties include acting with integrity, with independence and Jane must always act in a way that upholds the constitutional principle of the rule of law and the proper administration of justice.

Jane is not representing my conscience, and I do not need her to reflect my liberal sensibilities, but I do want her to do her job brilliantly because it means we have someone on the inside who we know must honour her duties as a regulated lawyer. We are very lucky to have her and the reassurance this brings that the rule of law and the administration of justice are cornerstones of each lawyer's role. In effect Jane is working for us too.

Does this mean Jane can always stop her employers from doing dumb things? No, but it certainly means that anything which looks illegal should be something that she is across, and it should be her final say whether it is legal or not. If the employer decides in good faith to do something that turns out to be illegal, then Jane cannot deny it happened or try to cover it up.

More sceptical readers may wonder if Jane can also use her training and ingenuity to find elaborate ways to avoid complying with inconvenient regulations. In my view, empathically, NO. The ice on that particular frozen pond is far too thin for a lawyer like Jane to skate on.

Jane is therefore a vital cog in the governance gears of each and every company that employs her. The protection this affords, is for us too.

However, what if the organisation that employs Jane is not a great place to work? What if her newly appointed Chief Executive doesn't like her, so he drops her from his direct reports and then from the executive committee; and he asks her to find costs savings by reducing her team from ten to six. Let's also suppose that Jane's partner has just been made redundant, and Jane has been to see her GP who says she is low and risks burnout, and now her dear old mum has been diagnosed with dementia.

To say the least, Jane is no longer in a supportive environment and her personal life is obviously fragile. She is incredibly vulnerable and any ethical pressure coming from her employer now will feel heightened and more uncomfortable, and she may not even be in the room to have her say.

This is not about whether Jane is about to act unethically, but it is about whether Jane can be at her best, and we should all want her to be at her best. I wouldn't want an exhausted, over-burdened and bullied surgeon to operate on me, and I don't want Jane to feel alone, disheartened and unsupported either.

Jane is a strong and resilient soul with an exemplary career; we might hope therefore that the regulator would want to help her. However, if she takes a specific concern to her regulator, I doubt she will feel supported. There is a confidential helpline which Jane can call for guidance, but most likely the regulator will recite the rules, tell her they don't regulate her CEO and suggest she resigns if it is all bit tricky. Not so much an ethics helpline, more an ethics hey-ho line.

So, in Jane's sunnier days we are all super grateful for her work and the rules that she works by. When it turns uncomfortable however, she is alone with a clueless regulator and a heightened risk that she will miss something that will reflect poorly on her and undermine the protection we all want from those important rules. We need a better way because this impacts us all.

Do we need new rules? No, I think the rules are great.

Do we need a more interested regulator? Yes, because if the regulator has Jane's back, we are all better for it. Waiting for her to leave, or fail, does not serve anyone's interests.

Should employers be allowed to undermine the rules by making it harder for Jane to comply with them? Obviously not, but some will, and we know they will.

This is not Jane's fault, and it is not fair to expect Jane to fix it on her own. Jane is potentially our justice hero and we need to protect her role. We also need to let her know that we care about the importance of her role. We need Jane and Jane needs us.

When things go wrong, in very rare cases the lawyers involved are incompetent or complicit fools, and shame on them when that is the case; however it is much more likely that we will find someone like Jane, and then the shame is on all of us.

November 2021

"Let those who feel the breath of sadness, sit down next to me"

My friend wanted to tell me about something that was happening at his work. Let's call him James.

He is responsible for delivering a significant project and had a talented team of colleagues from across the business working on it. One team member, let's call her Emma, worked in another division and although she was the most junior person on the project, she was responsible for delivering a key part of it. James was getting a little concerned about progress and decided to call her to see if all was well.

He described to me how Emma began to cry within a second of him asking if she was ok. This was not a tearful snuffle; this was a full-on emotional release. He told me how the sound of her sobbing will stay with him for a long time.

Nothing in work should make people feel like this.

The project was time critical and vital for the organisation to get right. It had reached an important milestone, and Emma held the key to it progressing. Emma knew this too and felt the weight of responsibility. She had been asking for help, but she felt unsupported, overwhelmed and unable to do any of her other work, in respect of which others were now complaining.

James tried to reassure her. He told her that none of this was her fault and that he would deal with it. He asked her to do one thing which was to email or call him every day, so that he knew she was doing ok.

James then told me about three conversations he had with colleagues about Emma.

He spoke first to the HR business partner for her division. He told James that it was a line management issue and that managers should follow the well-being policy. He also said however that it was an important project and some stress was inevitable. Maybe Emma could take a little break once the project was finished.

James then spoke to her line manager, who was more than a little grumpy that Emma had spoken to James. He said "if she feels overloaded, she should speak to me." He also said that it was a stressful project for everyone and that he couldn't make exceptions for one person and not do it for everyone. James asked him to speak to Emma today to see what could be done. When James checked with Emma two days later, she had not heard from anyone.

Unhappy with both these responses, James decided to speak to his Executive colleague (and peer) who ran the division where Emma and her line manager worked. James told her that he had spoken to HR and the line manager, but that he was unconvinced they were gripped of the need to help Emma. He said he was very worried for her well-being and just talking to her might be helpful. The response was non-committal and she reiterated that there was a well-being policy, and that she had confidence in the line manager. Perhaps Emma had over-reacted.

James knew of course that he was stepping on toes, but in his words "Emma needed someone to do something now, even just to talk to her, and if they won't, I will."

James reminded Emma to let him know each day how she was feeling and what action was being taken to support her. James promised he would step in again if nothing happened within a couple of days.

Shortly after Emma was given the support she needed, she completed her tasks and the project progressed well.

Reflecting on the story I know it may divide opinion, but I believe James did exactly the right thing. We must never put convention or policy in the way of doing the right thing for someone in distress.

Leadership is not easy and there isn't a playbook. James may have runkled a few relationships, but choosing not to act would have made him part of the problem. And, for goodness sake, what is the point of having a well-being policy if it means we can ignore someone literally crying out for help?

James told me that he may not have acted in this way a few years ago. Instead, he would have deferred to convention, showed sympathy, but not pushed for action. I noted with him that none of us become leaders by appointment. We become leaders by our actions.

James is a friend and I love him dearly, but I respect him more than ever. For some it might appear to be a minor moment in the rough and tumble of corporate life, but for me this is a defining example of how we all need to be. Emma, I suspect, will never forget what James did for her, and one day she will do the same for people that she can help. This is how we make our difference.

Let those who feel the breath of sadness sit down next to you.

Let your talent and potential wrap their arms around you

The ideal career appears to be a highly curated timeline of elegantly held roles, on an always upwards trajectory, with greater and greater reward on each and every gilded step.

And yet we know, those of us who are at the far end of the journey, that this is a mirage of airbrushed unreality. Careers are not Instagram posts of perfect moments. Careers are recipe-free concoctions of luck, opportunity, hard work and talent. Nothing is permanent, perfect or predictable.

Someone I spoke to recently said he would stay in his role, even though he was bored of it and conventional thinking would suggest he should move. He said that if he moved it would just be "the same old crap plot, but with a different set of broken characters."

Someone else I spoke to this week, who will start a new role in the New Year, is absolutely thrilled to have a new opportunity to start again. She has been worn down by a workplace that has only ever focussed on the next deal with an intensity that always takes her energy for granted, but never replaces it for her.

Both these calls were with brilliant people with CVs to die for, yet both had also been diminished by the attritional take-take-take of the workplace. Their conclusions were different, but we can all relate to the narrative.

The soft-focus on-line gurus may disagree, but my advice is to pack away any expectation that we can pilot our talent from one glamorous destination to another relying on a professional headshot, some mighty buzzwords and the faint whiff of entitlement based on the years we have worked beyond the date we qualified.

If we want to have a career that is good for us, our families, our wellbeing and the businesses we work in, I have some questions to reflect on and explore:

Are you prepared to change the way you behave, because personal growth is about what you can change, not what you can amplify.

Can you challenge without creating mistrust or extra stress for others?

Are you kind?

Do you live your values at work, or are they orphans to a quiet life of expediency?

Would you consider a sideways move (or even a step back) to learn something new?

Can you express your needs in ways that others can help you to meet them?

Can you describe the difference you have made?

How have you helped others to succeed?

Do you share unconditionally?

Can you describe your story with colour and joy and grace in a compelling way?

Your career path will most likely not be a stroll down a floodlit red carpet to an Oscar style retirement speech. It is more likely to be a yomping slog across a muddy field in the wrong shoes with an unhelpful commentary from your inner critic. Even so, I would love you to relish the journey, to live your story in the moment and to let your talent and potential wrap their arms around you.

Time to be the bold architects of our future, not the tenants of our past

As we tentatively move into a new age of seeing the world as something to be nurtured and not exploited, and as we need to find more certain and comprehensive ways to collaborate rather than just compete, it is time to be the bold architects of our future contribution, not the tenants of our past. As part of this reflection what should be the role of General Counsel?

Now, more than ever, at all the significant intersections between governance, technology, business, politics, sustainability, contracts, human rights and ethicality, there are lawyers. As societal, environmental and humanitarian expectations evolve, I do not think it is contentious to suggest that the purpose of lawyers should be abundantly clear for all to see, to understand and to evaluate.

The most senior employed lawyer on the payroll is the General Counsel. The vast majority of these lawyers undertake their roles for their institutions with great care, expertise and commitment. Many of us who observe them closely find their responsibilities daunting and their determination inspiring. It is a vital role, a pivotal role and a role that carries daily onerous challenges. We should therefore have the highest expectation that the role of General Counsel will be fulfilled with care, skill and courage.

I believe three things encourage and support this expectation:

First, and above all, that the rule of law and the administration of justice must never be comprised by what we do or choose not to do.

Second, that our role is never just as a servant to the expedient needs of a few executives temporarily in charge for now.

Third that in serving the best interests of the organisations we advise, we should self-consciously consider the impact of our actions on others including colleagues, suppliers, customers, the communities in which they trade and the environmental impact our businesses have on our planet.

However, fine words alone are not enough, we need to look at behaviours too. This is where we need to be especially clear because I believe we have allowed the conflation of ideas and behaviours that create an ambiguity and a tension with the purposefulness of the role I have just described.

- Are we gatekeepers or facilitators?
- Are we cheerleaders or critical friends?
- Are we commercial players or governance guardians?
- Are we pushers of envelopes or protectors of established best practice?
- Are we a consigliere to the CEO or our conscience?
- Do we lead opinion on doing the right thing or simply hope that we are all on the same page?
- Do we see our career as illuminated by the brands that employ us, or by the difference we make to the people and communities impacted by our work?
- If we see bad things, are we there to sweep up the mess as discreetly as possible, or to shine a light?
- Are we lawyers first and always, or are we business people with legal skills?

Many General Counsel will feel they can do all of these things, and move seamlessly between them, but my reflection is that these ambiguities are ultimately unhelpful. Where do we put the emphasis? Are we certain we will be on the right side of the line when the cold light of hindsight's scrutiny falls on our work. To borrow the Warren Buffet quote about the banks, "Only when the tide goes out do you discover who's been swimming naked."

My reflection is that if General Counsel want to be on the right side of history, now is the time to be leading the conversation that puts the role at the front and centre of new thinking. Not to accuse or diminish, but to emphatically leave behind the age of foggy ambiguity and move with certainty and determination to an age of transparent ethicality.

We need clarity of purpose and a conversation that frames an accountable contribution. I do not think we need more regulation to do this and we are not all trundling to hell in a hand-cart, but we should be open to small steps that are determined and impactful changes of emphasis. For example:

This might mean ensuring that the contracts made by our businesses are stripped of overbearing clauses and will instead reflect a desire to be fair, balanced and proportionate with respect to the legitimate interests of the organisations, places and people impacted by our agreements.

It might mean that we conduct disputes and litigation wholly on the merits of the issues and not tactically to exploit market position or financial power or to deflect reputational harm.

It might mean that when an employee complains of bullying, discrimination or harassment that we see our role not as the company's lawyer come what may, but as ensuring the company does the right thing.

It might mean that we do not hide bad actions under the cover of confidentiality clauses and that we expose wrongdoing.

It should mean that we are not complicit in strategies of distraction where poor behaviours are hidden from view for the sake of reputational risk management.

It might mean that we self-certify to our regulator on the renewal of our practicing certificates that we have complied with our code of professional conduct.

It might mean that our incentives are linked to our accountabilities as lawyers and not to commercial targets driven by sales, growth and market share.

It might mean taking a leading role in promoting the values of our organisations with our supply chain, our customers and with the communities in which we trade, so that these are embedded in our environmental policies, terms of trading and supply change management.

It should mean having a positive, active working relationship with all non-executive directors and perhaps a reporting line that is not just to an executive colleague, but additionally and explicitly to the chair of the Audit Committee.

It should mean a duty to report to the Board as soon as possible any instances of significant regulatory breach.

It might also mean some employment contract protection for us, so that if things look really bad, we have better options than to resign in professional silence or take a period of sick leave to lick our mental health wounds.

It might mean only using law firms that help us fulfil these responsibilities and who understand that these are duties we have been employed to discharge.

It should mean we are not nervous when a regulator or a judge asks for our papers, because legal professional privilege is a gift that should be used to serve justice and not to salve our employer's embarrassment.

I may be wrong, I often am, but we are undoubtedly moving to an age of seeing the world as something to be nurtured and not exploited. A world where collaboration will become increasingly important and where doing the right thing will always be more important than expediency. A time therefore to reflect and to be the bold architects of our future contribution, not the tenants of our past.

Twelve gifts of leadership

In the last few days, I have heard stories from and about all kinds of leaders. I have heard about ignorant and hurtful leadership, of confusing and missing-the-point leadership, but also of wonderfully inspiring and caring leadership. In time I would like to share more about all of this, but for now I want to dwell on the latter, as this was truly a gift in my week. It also made me wonder, especially at this time of year, if I could describe twelve gifts of leadership that I (rather than your true love) might give to you.

Listen beautifully
Listening is not about letting someone talk, or offering tea and sympathy. It isn't about having a rattling good conversation, or trying to jolly someone along. It isn't just saying that you have "an open door". The purpose of listening beautifully is to create a personal, calm and kind space for someone else to be heard by you. A peaceful place devoid of all distractions where feelings may rest. In such a place we all learn to trust and grow.

Sometimes turn your hierarchy upside down
In work we tend to spend most of our time with our direct reports and those we report to. Structure is important, but hierarchy can limit access rather than facilitate it. We should therefore make time to be with different people, to make different connections in our world of work, to learn new stories and see more clearly the talent and goodness all around us.

Trust your teams

No one comes to work to fail. Everyone hopes to succeed. It follows that nearly all failure is a failure of leadership. If we have recruited well, communicated clearly and resourced fairly, we have the building blocks in place for our teams to succeed; now we must trust our teams to do the right thing, because they almost certainly will. Growth and innovation, creativity and kindness will happen when we free people to make their difference, rather than constraining them to do as they are told.

Know that no matter what you say, it is your actions that define your values

Leadership is not easy, and there are so many different ways to be effective and to succeed (and to fail), but if we want to be remembered as a leader, it is as well to know that there are only two types of memorable leader, those who we would rather forget and those who we hope will remember us too.

Involve your colleagues, don't just include them

Even with the best of intentions we can be inclusive and still leave people feeling uncertain of their role, their value, and their right to belong. We must go beyond inclusion and allow people to feel involved. A well intended written policy can encourage inclusion, but only leaders can make people feel involved.

Make your purpose to make a difference to peoples' lives

I spoke to someone this week who lifted my heart. For some months she had been negotiating a pay review for her team. She had been in her leadership role for only a year, but she knew her team was underpaid. She went out on a limb, fought her case and prevailed. One of her colleagues receiving her pay award said that the difference it would make to her was "literally life-changing." How wonderful is that? I would love for us all to be able to put such moments on our CVs; they would say so much more about us than just another job title.

Make looking after your mental health an example for everyone to follow

Even if we do not feel vulnerable, some in our teams probably will. We must allow space for thoughts and cares and words, but most of all we must show the way and be the example others can follow. We should sometimes leave the office early, take all our holiday entitlement and not send work emails that will intrude on family time. We coach with our actions far more than we will ever coach with our words.

Be open about your weaknesses and ask for help

The first time I heard my chief executive say he was not sure what to do was the first time I truly respected his role. In work we talk a lot about delegation as a sign of good leadership; while this is true, implicit in delegation is that we know what to do, it's just that we are too busy to do it. It is even more valuable and important to talk about what we cannot do and to let our teams help us with this too. Breaking the "we know best" infallibility myth of leadership is another true gift.

Talk less but always speak well

Never be careless with your words. By way of example, I heard this week about a leader challenging her people to "get on the bus or be left behind". She may have thought it sounded like a rallying call worthy of St Crispin's Day, but buzzword bingo isn't leadership. Communication is sometimes an issue even in the best run businesses, but it is always a failure of leadership if we create ambiguity, mistrust, doubt and fear. We do not always have to inspire, it is still truly a gift of leadership if our words are thoughtful, consistent and clear.

Ask how you can help others to thrive

It is perhaps the most important question a leader ever asks. In my view it is the only question a leader needs to ask. "What do you need from me to help you succeed?"

Celebrate behaviours as well as achievements

Targets matter of course, but behaviours matter more. If we help to build a culture where people are valued, creative, and productive, where kindness is obvious and where everyone's story matters, I am certain the numbers will follow. Let's celebrate the culture we make, not just the business we generate.

Leave well, having made your difference

When you leave make sure you leave well. It is the last gift that you will share with the teams you have helped to become a vibrant, kind and creative collation of talents fulfilling their potential to make things better. Always leave well.

These are my twelve gifts of leadership, please feel you can open them early and share (although I have kept the receipts in case you don't like them!)

December 2021

The last note

This is my last blog of 2021 and it is a more personal reflection than I am typically comfortable to post, however I would like to tell you a little about how this year has felt for me. I hope it does not seem too self-indulgent.

I am not widely read or very sophisticated in my literary experiences, but I love the power of words to move people. There is a poem by William Butler Yeats that always moves me and it has become increasingly important in a year that has pulled the heart out of my work, our plans and our hopes to even carry on.

> "Had I the heavens' embroidered cloths,
> Enwrought with golden and silver light,
> The blue and the dim and the dark cloths
> Of night and light and the half-light,
> I would spread the cloths under your feet:
> But I, being poor, have only my dreams;
> I have spread my dreams under your feet;
> Tread softly because you tread on my dreams."

For the last two decades my dream has been to play a small part in shaping a kinder, more thoughtful and more generous profession. My style is not to stand at the front and shout, and I prefer quiet anonymity as the place for my best work. I have always believed however that to succeed I must spread this dream beneath your feet and ask that we tread softly together. It is one of the reasons that I write, because it means I can place my words here for you to read, while I quietly withdraw, leaving you with my words in peace.

Like lots of people who have taken their own path, I do not consider that I have a job, or even a career; what I have is a chance to make my difference in my way. All was well until the world changed in March 2020. Within a few weeks old certainties became fragile and existential concerns filled our minds. Now we know that hundreds of thousands of people have died, families have been kept apart, and nearly everyone has at sometime felt overwhelmed with feelings of sadness, regret and of visceral loss.

As 2020 became 2021, the long winter gripped my hopes for a year of recovery and shook them from my grasp. I could feel my dreams slipping through my fingers and I observed how my business could freefall from the sky. I have never felt more lost or helpless, or less able to ask for help knowing the world was convulsed by far more dreadful fears than my own.

Dreams however are hard to kill. When we wrap them in hope, our dreams never really leave us.

Back in February 2020, we had started a leadership programme that should have finished in March that year. Thanks to Covid, it had to be postponed and this programme became, for me at least, a hanging symbol of hopes frozen and dreams locked down.

Then, last month, twenty months after it began, we met again to finish what we had started. The words of W B Yeats were with me on the first evening of the reconvened programme. That night we had the privilege to work with the London Mozart Players and in a room where delegates and musicians gathered, we heard the joy of beautiful sounds made just for us. There was a blissful moment when the last note was played and it seemed to borrow the stillness of our listening to glide perfectly into silence. Those of us in the room knew that nothing mattered more in that moment than for our stillness to be the respectful accompaniment for this precious sound; the sound of a single note coming to rest and becoming a gift for us of a small, but perfect memory.

I knew then that my dream was still alive. If a single note in a frantic world of crashing discordant noise could leave such a deep impression and evoke feelings that will last long after the note itself has gone, imagine what caring notes we might leave in the memories of those who hear our words?

We may never have access to heavens' embroidered cloths, enwrought with golden and silver light, but even when we are poor, we are still more valuable and more important and more influential than we could ever imagine.

In 2021 my business nearly died. Accountants would have declared "nothing to see here," but my dreams are not on any balance sheet, and I am the luckiest man in the world to work with people who tread softly with me. My words today therefore are for my extraordinary Faculty and for the delegates who literally stayed the course. With all my heart, thank you.

In 2022 we will build again, working for that kinder, more thoughtful and more generous profession once more, one day at a time and grateful for every day.

I hope 2022 may bring you love and safety, kindness and opportunity. May you feel you can unfurl your dreams, and if you are lucky enough to spread your dreams at the feet of others, please ask them to tread softly with you.

Other books by Paul

All these books can
be bought from the
LBC Wise Counsel website:
www.lbcwisecounsel.com